Customer Relationship Management in Electronic Markets

Customer Relationship Management in Electronic Markets has been co-published simultaneously as *Journal of Relationship Marketing,* Volume 2, Numbers 3/4 2003.

Customer Relationship Management in Electronic Markets

Gopalkrishnan R. Iyer, PhD
David Bejou, PhD
Editors

Customer Relationship Management in Electronic Markets has been co-published simultaneously as *Journal of Relationship Marketing,* Volume 2, Numbers 3/4 2003.

Routledge
Taylor & Francis Group
New York   London

First published by

Best Business Books®, 10 Alice Street, Binghamton, NY 13904-1580 USA

Best Business Books® is an imprint of The Haworth Press, Inc., 10 Alice Street, Binghamton, NY 13904-1580 USA.

This edition published 2013 by Routledge

Routledge
Taylor & Francis Group
711 Third Avenue
New York, NY 10017

Routledge
Taylor & Francis Group
2 Park Square, Milton Park
Abingdon, Oxon OX14 4RN

Routledge is an imprint of the Taylor & Francis Group, an informa business

Customer Relationship Management in Electronic Markets has been co-published simultaneously as *Journal of Relationship Marketing,* Volume 2, Numbers 3/4 2003.

The development, preparation, and publication of this work has been undertaken with great care. However, the publisher, employees, editors, and agents of The Haworth Press and all imprints of The Haworth Press, Inc., including The Haworth Medical Press® and The Pharmaceutical Products Press®, are not responsible for any errors contained herein or for consequences that may ensue from use of materials or information contained in this work. Opinions expressed by the author(s) are not necessarily those of The Haworth Press, Inc.

Cover design by Brooke R. Stiles

Library of Congress Cataloging-in-Publication Data

Customer relationship management in electronic markets / Gopalkrishnan R. Iyer, David Bejou, editors.
    p. cm.
Co-published simultaneously as Journal of Relationship Marketing, Volume 2, Numbers 3/4 2003. Includes bibliographical references and index.
    ISBN 0-7890-1944-2 (hard cover : alk. paper) – ISBN 0-7890-1945-0 (soft cover : alk. paper)
1. Customer relations–Management. 2. Customer relations–Technological innovations. 3. Electronic commerce. I. Iyer, Gopalkrishnan R. II. Bejou, David. III. Journal of Relationship Marketing (Binghamton, N.Y.)

HF5415.5.C843 2004
658.8'12'02854678–dc22
                                                                            2003026667

Customer Relationship Management in Electronic Markets

CONTENTS

ABOUT THE EDITORS

Gopalkrishnan R. Iyer, PhD, Guest Editor, is the InternetCoast Institute Adams Professor of Industry Studies in the Department of Marketing at The Florida Atlantic University (FAU) in Boca Raton, Florida. He has taught at Virginia Tech, Baruch College (City University of New York), ESIC (Spain), and Dartmouth College, and has conducted executive seminars on various topics in diverse locations. His industry experience includes strategic management positions with two of Asia's Top 50 multinational corporations.

Dr. Iyer's current research interests are in the areas of international business, business-to-business marketing, e-business, entrepreneurship, and the Hollywood film industry. His research has been published, among other outlets, in the *Journal of International Business Studies*, the *Journal of International Marketing*, the *Journal of Business Research, Psychology and Marketing*, the *Journal of Business Ethics*, the *Journal of Business-to-Business Marketing*, the *Journal of Business & Industrial Marketing*, and the *Journal of East-West Business*. His recent book projects include editing *Marketing Challenges in Transition Economies* (1999) and *Teaching International Business: Ethics and Corporate Social Responsibility* (2000).

David Bejou, PhD, is Professor of Marketing and Dean of School of Business at Virginia State University. He previously served on the faculty of the University of North Carolina at Wilmington, where he was nominated in 1996 for the Chancellor Teaching Excellence Award, and nominated in both 1995 and 1996 for the Faculty Scholarship Award. He has also been a faculty member at several other universities in the United States and Australia.

Dr. Bejou has published widely in professional journals, including the *Journal of Services Marketing*, the *Journal of Business Research*, the *Journal of Marketing Management*, the *International Journal of Bank Marketing*, and the *European Journal of Marketing*. He is a member of the American Marketing Association and the Academy of Marketing Science, and has been a presenter or Session Chair at many national and international conferences.

Dr. Bejou has served as a marketing/promotions consultant to the United Carolina Bank (UCB), Brunswick Community College, and other businesses and community organizations.

Preface

This special volume focuses on "Customer Relationship Management in Electronic Markets." Despite the lackluster performance of most firms over the Internet, firms either providing CRM technologies or implementing them properly are doing brisk business. The importance of forming long-term relationships in today's economy does not need detailed and convincing arguments. However, the approaches to obtaining loyalty in electronic markets and forging profitable ties with customers over a technological interface are many and varied. This publication provides some strong conceptual frameworks elaborating the various issues in developing and implementing CRM in both B2B and B2C markets.

In the introductory article, Gopalkrishnan R. Iyer and I discuss the various challenges that arise from simply assuming that CRM programs would work as intended and outline the various issues firms must consider when implementing technology-based CRM strategies. In the next article, Shelby H. McIntyre argues that eCRM in e-tailing must focus on several important and inter-related issues, including considering the relational needs of online customers and striving for providing satisfaction and building relational commitment. Dhruv Grewal, Joan Lindsey-Mullikin and Jeanne Munger then present a conceptual framework that explores the antecedents and consequences of loyalty in e-tailing. While the preceding two articles focus primarily on B2C markets, the next two articles focus on B2B markets. Kishore Gopalakrishna Pillai and Arun Sharma emphasize the critical role of forming and maintaining relationships in varied B2B exchanges. J. David Lichtenthal examines how the Internet could be seamless integrated in the buyer-seller relationship and develops a framework for business buyer relationship management (BBRM). In the final article of the special volume, Jon M. Shapiro,

[Haworth co-indexing entry note]: "Preface." Bejou, David. Co-published simultaneously in *Journal of Relationship Marketing* (Best Business Books, an imprint of The Haworth Press, Inc.) Vol. 2, No. 3/4, 2003, pp. xxi-xxii; and: *Customer Relationship Management in Electronic Markets* (ed: Gopalkrishnan R. Iyer, and David Bejou) Best Business Books, an imprint of The Haworth Press, Inc., 2003, pp. xiii-xiv. Single or multiple copies of this article are available for a fee from The Haworth Document Delivery Service [1-800-HAWORTH, 9:00 a.m. - 5:00 p.m. (EST). E-mail address: docdelivery@haworthpress.com].

Nicholas C. Romano, Jr. and Banwari Mittal adopt a customer centric view in evaluating the various information technology (IT) mediated interactions in the buyer-seller relationship.

Conceptualized and executed at a time when there is less "hype" surrounding either the Internet and when the Internet is simply becoming a part and parcel of everyday business life, this special volume offers conceptual models and frameworks that have gained considerably from past theories and realities. Good theories and models endure volatile changes in realities, and I am confident that the articles in this special volume will guide academic research and managerial implementation of CRM in the years to come.

David Bejou, PhD
Founding Editor
Journal of Relationship Marketing

Customer Relationship Management in Electronic Markets

Gopalkrishnan R. Iyer

Florida Atlantic University

David Bejou

Virginia State University

SUMMARY. Customer relationship management, or CRM, has found increased attention in both the academic and managerial worlds of marketing in recent years. While the Internet has greatly enabled the application of CRM in fostering loyal customers, the preliminary results on the effectiveness and efficiency of technology-based CRM has been far from discouraging. The authors identify various contentious issues behind the various key concepts of relationship management and identify several areas that deserve closer academic scrutiny and managerial inspection. The paper also comments on the extent to which Internet technology can bring about closer relationships with a firm's customers. *[Article copies available for a fee from The Haworth Document Delivery Service: 1-800-HAWORTH. E-mail address: <docdelivery@haworthpress.com> Website: <http://www.HaworthPress. com> © 2003 by The Haworth Press, Inc. All rights reserved.]*

Gopalkrishnan R. Iyer, PhD, is InternetCoast Institute Adams Professor of Industry Studies, Department of Marketing, Florida Atlantic University, 777 Glades Road, Boca Raton, FL 33431.

David Bejou, PhD, is Professor of Marketing and Dean of School of Business, Virginia State University, Petersburg, VA 23806.

Gopalkrishnan R. Iyer thanks the InternetCoast Institute Adams Professorship for support for this paper.

[Haworth co-indexing entry note]: "Customer Relationship Management in Electronic Markets." Iyer, Gopalkrishnan R., and David Bejou. Co-published simultaneously in *Journal of Relationship Marketing* (Best Business Books, an imprint of The Haworth Press, Inc.) Vol. 2, No. 3/4, 2003, pp. 1-13; and: *Customer Relationship Management in Electronic Markets* (ed: Gopalkrishnan R. Iyer, and David Bejou) Best Business Books, an imprint of The Haworth Press, Inc., 2003, pp. 1-13. Single or multiple copies of this article are available for a fee from The Haworth Document Delivery Service [1-800-HAWORTH, 9:00 a.m. - 5:00 p.m. (EST). E-mail address: docdelivery@ haworthpress.com].

1

KEYWORDS. Customer relationship management (CRM), e-CRM, electronic market relationships, relationship marketing

INTRODUCTION

Very few topics within marketing, both among academics and practitioners, have elicited so much interest and attention as that of the benefits and strategies for a firm in forming long-term relationships with its key customers. Long ignored in favor of strategies and tactics whereby marketing managers could increase their market share, the issues of enhancing customer satisfaction and thereby, customer loyalty and retention, found increasing prominence in both the academic and managerial worlds of marketing in the U.S. only in the 1990s. While most of the initial discussions and strategic activities in building long-term relationships focused mainly on business-to-business marketing and services relationships, the past few years have witnessed a veritable renaissance in the study and application of these approaches to the field of business-to-consumer relationships (Anderson Håkånsson and Johanson 1994; Berry 1995; Ford 1990; Grönroos 1994).

Two of the most prominent developments in the last several years have been the expansion of Internet-based transactions and customer relationship management (Sheth and Sisodia 2001). The nexus of the two, or customer relationship management in electronic markets, has received increasing prominence both in the academic and trade treatments of the subject as well as in business adoption of customer relationship management (CRM) technologies (Rigby, Reichheld and Schefter 2002). However, the outlook for the continued emphasis on CRM, whether primarily web-based or implemented using multiple processes and technologies, remains one of cautious optimism. While businesses have rushed to adopt CRM, spending millions on technology and its adoption, recent research suggests that the promised profitability increases are yet to be obtained (Rigby, Reichheld and Schefter 2002).

What has gone wrong in the rush to adopt CRM technologies and implement CRM programs? Were academics misguided by presumptions about relationship marketing? Or, were business executives seeking an alchemy that did not exist? This paper traces the core assumptions behind the key concepts in customer relationship management and identifies several areas that deserve closer scrutiny. The paper also comments on the extent to which technology can bring about closer relationships with a firm's customers.

APPROACHES TO CRM

In general, relationship marketing subsumes a variety of strategic approaches ranging from micro-segmentation of customer markets, management of data on identified and identifiable customer characteristics and behaviors, mass customization, continual learning and adaptation of marketing strategy with changing customer needs, and the creation of sustainable competitive advantages based on stronger ties with one's customers. The obvious advantages of relationship marketing are in terms of the ability to charge a price premium for satisfying unique customer needs, lower costs of retaining current customers compared to those of procuring newer ones, and the ability to retain one's customers in mature markets despite competitive onslaught. The less obvious, though relevant, organizational advantages are in terms of the reduction of demand uncertainty, profiting from the mutual interdependence between the firm and the customer, and the long-term sustainability of the organization itself.

This broad approach to relationship marketing finds somewhat different applications in business-to-business (B2B) versus business-to-consumer (B2C) markets. In B2B markets, the importance of creating strategic partnerships and alliances and obtaining long-term commitment with suppliers and distributors is emphasized (Iyer 2003). In B2C markets, micro-segmentation and specific targeting are stressed along with an emphasis on various monetary and non-monetary value creation approaches. Further, the different approaches to CRM in B2B versus B2C markets are driven by the assumed (and, often real) differences between the nature of these markets, the types of buyer-seller relationships that are sought, and degree to which the overall relationship is guided by a long-term contract.

It is also recognized that CRM is a process, and as such can be understood either in terms of distinct phases of the relationships or in terms of the strategic steps that need to be undertaken to achieve relationship objectives (Heide 1994; Winer 2001). The process can be summarized to include four stages of the buyer-seller relationship: identification of relationship partners; development of the relationship; maintenance of the relationship; and re-evaluation of the relationship or its termination. The strategic steps, on the other hand, may include: customer/segment identification; customer targeting; relationship marketing and management; and, the evaluation of the relationship and firm performance. B2B researchers prefer to understand CRM in terms of its process stages, while B2C researchers frequently conceptualize CRM in terms of its strategic activities. As such, the focus in B2B relationships appears to be centered around the development of long-term relationships through building trust and commitment among the exchange partners. On other hand, a central role is given to the development of loyal customers in B2C relationships.

While the CRM priorities appear to be different in B2B versus B2C relationships, closer inspection would reveal that their aims are the same. Both attempt to create a small numbers situation between the firm and the customer (or supplier) in otherwise competitive markets, and both seek enhanced profitability as the end-result of CRM activities.

CRM AND THE INTERNET

The Internet has been both a boon and a bane for customer relationship management. On one hand, the lowered costs of market entry (or the creation of an additional communication and/or sales channel) increases the competition for customer attention and sales, while concurrently reducing seller margins through reductions in buyer search costs as well (Varadarajan and Yadav 2002). This places additional pressures on firms to seek out their most valuable customers and devise programs and strategies to retain them. Fortunately, the Internet also helps firms pursue such objectives. Firms can now understand customer needs better, develop more customer-centric programs for satisfying needs, and offer enhanced value through managing customer information and needs, and providing customized products and services (Iyer, Miyazaki, Grewal and Giordano 2002; Sheth, Sisodia and Sharma 2000).

The Internet as a technological tool adds greater value to CRM, primarily through making the various stages/strategies of CRM more cost-efficient as well as enabling a host of other activities that would have otherwise been either impossible or arduous (Greenberg 2002). The Internet enables ready identification of the customer/visitor, cost-efficient data collection, personalization, customization, and interactivity in the CRM process. These enhanced value-creating activities also expand the abilities of firms to "establish, nurture, and sustain long-term customer relationships than ever before" (Winer 2001, p. 89).

While traditional CRM activities remained distinct from web-enabled CRM, or e-CRM, in the early years of the "dot-com" era, it is being increasingly recognized that web-enabled CRM is now the norm rather than the exception (Greenberg 2002). This is due to the fact that most firms now view the Internet as an additional channel either for communication or sales, or both, and that firms are recognizing that open-standard Internet TCP/IP protocols, XML, and Internet telephony are not only cost-efficient but also enable better contacts with customers (Apte, Liu, Pednault and Smyth 2002). However, at the same time, CRM left completely to technology also has its drawbacks, most notably and ironically in the impersonal provision of a much-touted personalization.

Recent evidence suggests several failures in the adoption and implementation of CRM programs (Ebner, Hu, Levitt and McCrory 2002; Rigby, Reichheld and Schefter 2002; Ross and Weill 2002). In most cases, the failures have been due to an overt reliance on technology on the mistaken assumption that a high-tech solution contributes to better relationships than a low-tech one (Rigby, Reichheld and Schefter 2002). Other factors cited for the failure of CRM technologies include a lack of business vision, the lack of a comprehensive and *a priori* customer segmentation and relationship strategy, leaving corporate business and strategic marketing decisions to the information technology (IT) departments, and the failure to either suitably integrate or align organizational culture and incentives with the technology-based CRM (Ebner, Hu, Levitt and McCrory 2002; Rigby, Reichheld and Schefter 2002; Ross and Weill 2002).

But the core concern over technology-based CRM remains the inattention to human factors in the development and nurture of the buyer-seller relationship. These human factors go beyond the user-friendly design and deployment of CRM (Bressler 2001). It involves building and sustaining trust in the relationship, developing emotional and structural bonds with customers, and demonstrating sincerity and commitment in the relationship-all of which find only partial and imperfect solutions when left to technology alone. For example, Internet-based CRM approaches, while recognizing the importance of trust, view trust in the very limited context of providing and guaranteeing privacy and security when dealings with customers through websites (Keen, Balance, Chan and Schrump 1999; Winer 2001). This view of trust overlooks the tremendous complexity and sociological origins of the construct–one that was an integral part of the traditional approaches to relationship marketing. Moreover, how good can a guarantee of privacy be when the small print in most firms' websites states that they can change their privacy policy unilaterally at any time (see also Dowling 2002)?

At another level, both the popularity and increasing failures of CRM approaches could possibly be from the applications and misapplications, respectively, of the core linkages between customer satisfaction, loyalty, and firm profitability. It is widely held that a firm that seeks to consciously and programmatically satisfy customer needs–these needs could be quality of products and/or services, price, or value–would, of course, benefit from high satisfaction among its target group of customers. Satisfying target customers is key and the logical first step towards obtaining greater loyalty among customers (Reicheheld 1994). Loyal customers are more profitable to the firm since it costs less to retain them as compared with seeking new customers and less transaction costs are incurred in serving loyal customers. Further, they are more likely to increase revenues for the firm both by buying more as well as recommending the firm and/or its products/services more often (Reichheld 1993, 1994; Zeithaml, Rust and Lemon 2001).

The above model of the links between customer satisfaction, loyalty, and firm profitability is intuitive and appealing, which may contribute to academics and practitioners alike seeking ways to implement elements of the model rather than test the model *per se*. However, some research evidence and practical observations challenge the various elements of the presumed linkages. These are detailed below and mapped in Figure 1.

Links Between Drivers of Satisfaction and Customer Satisfaction. It is presumed that most firms know exactly what it takes to satisfy their core target group of customers. This in turn, rests on the presumption that firms know their best target group of customers. However, segmentation methods of aggregating customer preferences are often only the beginning of an attempt to study customers and not the end. First, traditional segmentation is quite disassociated with customer profitability

FIGURE 1. The Satisfaction-Loyalty-Profitability Link

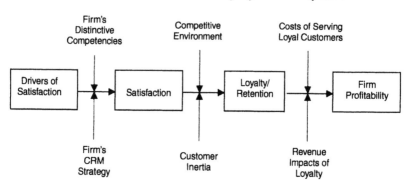

and/or the firm's ability, both in terms of costs and competence, in satisfying a target group of customers. Second, more sophisticated segmentation approaches, such as data mining, are based more on past customer behavior, missing out on a possible more appropriate base of customers or even the cognitive and intentional dimensions of current customers.

Traditional market research methods could be supplemented with other methods of assessing what current and potential future customers view critical to their consumption/adoption decisions. Moreover, traditional segmentation methods could be complemented with methods of assessing potential costs and profitability in serving each segment so as to select the best segment. But more immediately, the mere understanding of customer needs/preferences may not be enough; firms must carefully assess their distinctive competencies in providing the highest satisfaction levels for each driver of satisfaction for their target group of customers. The links between the various drivers of customer satisfaction and the firm's unique competence in providing the highest value for each of these drivers must be at the heart of the firm's CRM strategy (Burke 2002). For example, an Internet firm's CRM strategy may offer specific "best" customers additional values and services, such as web-based personalization, easy ordering, rewards for repeat purchases and larger orders, and so on, but if the core benefits sought by customers revolve around factors such as greater product information, timely delivery, and more post-sales support, the firm's CRM strategy may be missing the boat altogether.

Link Between Satisfaction and Loyalty/Retention. The link between satisfaction and customer loyalty, or retention, depends upon a number of assumptions. First, it is held that highly satisfied customers may not have the incentive or may not like to incur additional search costs in seeking out competing alternatives. For this reason, they are more likely to buy repeatedly from the same firm or consumer the same product or services and thus, exhibit loyalty. Second, highly satisfied customers would have incurred considerable "sunk costs" in learning, dealing, and using the current products/services, so that any other alternative would most likely involve higher switching costs as well. Third, highly satisfied customers are less likely to be swayed by price and other temporary incentives offered by competitors and are less likely to switch. Finally, highly satisfied customers develop stronger emotional and structural ties with the current firm and/or its products/services, and so any decision to switch is often more agonizing and therefore either postponed or avoided by the customer altogether.

However, empirical evidence on the link between satisfaction and loyalty is only mixed so far. The relationship is moderated by the nature of the product or service, type of industry, and competitive environment (Jones and Sasser 1995). Loyalty in Internet-based relationships is particularly difficult due to the highly competitive and new environments created, but also due to the fact that loyalty depends largely upon building trust–something that is proving to be quite difficult to achieve given the largely impersonal context of Internet-based transactions (Reichheld and Schefter 2000).

At another level, satisfied customers may remain loyal simply due to inertia (Reinartz and Kumar 2002). Better, and probably more satisfying alternatives may exist, but the customer may not wish to pursue these for a variety of reasons. These could range from perceptions–real or assumed–such as lower convenience, greater risks, lower privacy and security, higher search costs, and higher switching costs (Reichheld and Schefter 2000; Syzmanski and Hise 2000).

Firms attempting to craft their CRM strategies need to be cognizant of the factors that contribute to the link between satisfaction and loyalty for their specific firm/market/industry and for their specific product and service strategies.

Link Between Loyalty and Profitability. The link between loyalty and profitability is explained by the lower cost of serving loyal customers as well as the increases in revenue through increased patronage and positive word-of-mouth of such loyal customers. At the same time, it is also assumed that loyal customers are not price sensitive, thereby allowing firms to charge higher prices for added benefits and services provided to them. However, in empirical observations across four firms, each from a different industry, Reinartz and Kumar (2002) found very little support for the core assumptions behind the loyalty-profitability link. Selden and Colvin (2000) offer several reasons behind why a customer-centric strategy may not be contributing to higher profitability. These include: failure to capture the differences in profitability across difference sets of customer either due to denial or problems in measurement, wrong expectations about the profit impacts of new customers, assuming that all customers contribute almost equally to profits, problems with implementation, and problems in linking customer strategy to the firm's market value.

The bottom line, however, is that too little is known about the much-touted links between customer loyalty and profitability. Loyal customers expect reciprocal benefits from the firm, whether in B2B or B2C markets, and a firm's attempt to systematically gouge its own loyal customers through higher prices for added benefits or services that are not perceived to be really of value by the customer would be tantamount to killing the goose that lays golden eggs. CRM strategies must be based on a detailed evaluation of the loyalty-profitability link as well as the real nature of the bond between the firm and the customer (Sawhney and Zabin 2002).

CRM FOR THE NEXT GENERATION

The above discussion offers some issues that challenge the core assumptions upon which current CRM theories and strategies are built. Current CRM implementation through the Internet could also be evaluated through an examination of strategies/tactics that are well enabled by technology and others that may require more human and personal intervention. In this context, it is useful to make a distinction between a firm's transactional goals and its relational goals. As Jap and Mohr (2002) argue in the B2B context, the types of relationships expected and/or developed play an important part in how firms evaluate new opportunities, circumstances and emerging technologies. Incentive-based programs, such as frequency and loyalty programs, may serve to provide only transactional benefits, with the relational impact of such programs now increasingly taken to task (Dowling 2002; Dowling and Uncles 1997; Reinartz and Kumar 2002).

However, technology-based CRM programs may quite adequate for achieving such transactional goals. For example, customers in B2C markets may find Internet-based personalization for obtaining loyalty rewards, easy ordering, delivery tracking, and routine pre- and post-sales service support to be of value. Similarly, customers in B2B markets may find cost-efficiencies and value enhancements in routine purchases through B2B exchanges. On the other hand, a pure technology solution may be inadequate for several customer issues, including communication on critical issues, handling complaints, service recovery, and for developing trust and deeper structural ties. For example, in both work and non-work contexts, computer-mediated communications, such as e-mails, are perceived by users to be less valuable for developing social relationships as compared to offline communication methods, such as face-to-face contact and telephone conversations (Cummings, Butler, and Kraut 2002). Given that the primary CRM objective is to enable a long-term relationship with customers, it follows that the relational dimension and even some of the transactional dimensions of relationship building and maintenance would require the use of more personal, human contacts. Table 1 details some of the various business-customer relationships for which a technological solution could be primary and others for which human intervention may be needed. It could be noted that from Table 1 that traditional relationship marketing approaches that advocate relational goals and are based on development and nurture of trust and structural ties are quite distant from the CRM solutions offered simply through technology. Thus, the problems in the adoption and implementation of CRM technologies may not simply be from issues in the mismatch between the technology and the organization and culture in which it is to be embedded. Rather, the problems could lie in the fundamental conceptualization of customer relationship objectives as applicable more to *transactions* with customers, not *relationships* with customers. For technology-based CRM to be deployed successfully, it must be secondary to the personal, human relationships formed between the firm and its customers, at least until such time as a value migration occurs between the offline and online domains.

CONCLUSION

The challenges posed in the preceding sections are for both academics as well as practitioners alike. While practitioners need to re-evaluate their deployment of CRM technologies, especially their goals and the types of tasks for which technological solutions are particularly effective, academics must engage in a detailed empirical examination through

TABLE 1. Technological and Human Contact Requirements in e-CRM

Exchange Focus	Technology Solution Primary	Human Intervention Needed
Transactional Goals	* Facilitation of consumer search * Decision-making support for standardized products * Convenience in ordering * Delivery tracking * Limited personalization * Asynchronous electronic communication (E-mail) * Technical support for routine issues	* Personal contacts and communication * Handling non-routine service complaints * Service recovery * Complex decision-making aids
Relational Goals	* Understanding customer and segment needs unobtrusively (data mining) * Interactivity (synchronous communication, etc.) * Third party e-CRM * Enterprise Resource Planning	* Identity relations * Emotional bonding * Deeper, structural ties * Development and nurture of trust

replications and extensions of past studies of the satisfaction-loyalty-profitability links to draw out the boundary conditions under which these links hold true. Specifically, research needs to focus on:

- the conditions under which satisfaction contributes to loyalty;
- the extent and processes by which loyalty contributes to profitability, especially through greater research attention to marketing's impacts on financial results;
- how and when technology-based CRM approaches are appropriate in managing relationships with one's key customers; and
- relative differences in customer value provided for each firm-customer interaction when using online and offline methods.

While the death of relationship marketing has been prematurely forewarned elsewhere, the core philosophy of creating and sustaining a customer-centric organization has found more subscribers in recent years. However, the conceptualization, development, deployment and implementation of customer relationship management strategies are more challenging than simply installing and managing a technology infrastructure. Until such time as this is realized, CRM programs would appear to be either ineffective or remain quite cost-inefficient. It would also appear as if the skeptics were right, if only for the wrong reasons.

REFERENCES

Anderson, James C., Håkan Håkånsson and Jan Johanson (1994), "Dyadic Business Relationships Within a Business Network Context," *Journal of Marketing*, 58 (October), 1-15.

Apte, Chidanand, Bing Liu, Edwin P.D. Pednault and Padhraic Smyth (2002), "Business Applications of Data Mining," *Communications of the ACM*, 45 (August), 49-53.

Berry, Leonard L. (1995), "Relationship Marketing of Services–Growing Interest, Emerging Perspectives," *Journal of the Academy of Marketing Science*, 23 (Fall), 236-245.

Bressler, Martin (2001), "Internet CRM Must Have Human Touch," *Marketing News*, October 22, 42.

Burke, Raymond R. (2002), "Technology and the Customer Interface: What Consumers Want in the Physical and Virtual Store," *Journal of the Academy of Marketing Science*, 30 (Fall), 411-32.

Cummings, Jonathon N., Brian Butler and Robert Kraut (2002), "The Quality of Online Social Relationships," *Communications of the ACM*, 45 (July), 103-108.

Dowling, Grahame (2002), "Customer Relationship Management: In B2C Markets, Often Less Is More," *California Management Review*, 44 (Spring), 87-104.

Dowling, Grahame and Mark Uncles (1997), "Do Customer Loyalty Programs Really Work?" *Sloan Management Review*, 38 (Summer), 71-82.

Ebner, Manuel, Arthur Hu, Daniel Levitt and Jim McCrory (2002), "How to Rescue CRM," *McKinsey Quarterly*, 4, 48-57.

Ford, David (1990), *Understanding Business Markets: Interaction, Relationships, and Networks*. London: Academic Press.

Greenberg, Jeff (2002), *CRM at the Speed of Light: Capturing and Keeping Customers in Internet Real Time*, 2nd edition. Berkeley, CA: McGraw-Hill/Osborne.

Grönroos, Christian (1994), "From Marketing Mix to Relationship Marketing: Towards a Paradigm Shift in Marketing," *Management Decision*, 32 (2), 4-20.

Heide, Jan B. (1994), "Interorganizational Governance in Marketing Channels," *Journal of Marketing*, 58 (January), 71-85.

Iyer, Gopalkrishnan R., Anthony D. Miyazaki, Dhruv Grewal and Maria Giordano (2002), "Linking Web-Based Segmentation to Pricing Tactics," *Journal of Product and Brand Management*, 11 (5), 288-300.

Iyer, Gopalkrishnan R. (2003), "Internet-Enabled Linkages: Balancing Strategic Considerations with Operational Efficiencies in B-to-B Marketing," *Journal of Business-to-Business Marketing*, 11 (1/2), 35-59.

Jap, Sandy D. and Jakki J. Mohr (2002), "Leveraging Internet Technologies in B2B Relationships," *California Management Review*, 44 (Summer), 24-38.

Jones, Thomas O. and W. Earl Sasser, Jr. (1995), "Why Satisfied Customers Defect," *Harvard Business Review*, 73 (November-December), 88-99.

Keen, Peter, Craigg Ballance, Sally Chan, and Steve Schrump (1999), *Electronic Commerce Relationships: Trust By Design*. Upper Saddle River, NJ: Prentice Hall PTR.

Reichheld, Frederick F. (1993), "Loyalty-Based Management," *Harvard Business Review*, 71 (March-April), 64-73.

Reichheld, Frederick F. (1994), "Loyalty and the Renaissance of Marketing," *Marketing Management*, 2 (4), 10-21.

Reichheld, Frederick F. and Phil Schefter (2000), "E-Loyalty: Your Secret Weapon on the Web," *Harvard Business Review*, 78 (July-August), 105-113.

Reinartz, Werner and V. Kumar (2002), "The Mismanagement of Customer Loyalty," *Harvard Business Review*, 80 (July), 86-94.

Rigby, Darrell K., Frederick F. Reichheld and Phil Schefter (2002), "Avoid the Four Perils of CRM," *Harvard Business Review*, 80 (February), 101-109.

Ross, Jeanne W. and Peter Weill (2002), "Six IT Decisions Your IT People Shouldn't Make," *Harvard Business Review*, 80 (November), 84-91.

Sawhney, Mohanbir and Jeff Zabin (2002), "Managing and Measuring Relational Equity in the Network Economy," *Journal of the Academy of Marketing Science*, 30 (Fall), 313-32.

Selden, Larry and Geoffrey Colvin (2002), "Will This Customer Sink Your Stock?" *Fortune*, September 30, 126-132.

Sheth, Jagdish N. and Rajendra S. Sisodia (2001), "High Performance Marketing," *Marketing Management*, 10 (September/October), 18-23.

Sheth, Jagdish N., Rajenda S. Sisodia, and Arun Sharma (2000), "Antecedents and Consequences of the Growth of Customer-Centric Marketing," *Journal of the Academy of Marketing Science*, 28 (Winter), 55-66.

Syzmanksi, David M. and Richard T. Hise (2000), "e-Satisfaction: An Initial Examination," *Journal of Retailing*, 76 (3), 309-322.

Varadarajan, P. Rajan and Manjit S. Yadav (2002), "Marketing Strategy and the Internet: An Organizing Framework," *Journal of the Academy of Marketing Science*, 30 (Fall), 296-312.

Winer, Russell S. (2001), "A Framework for Customer Relationship Management," *California Management Review*, 43 (Summer), 89-105.

Zeithaml, Valerie A., Roland T. Rust, and Katherine N. Lemon (2001), "The Customer Pyramid: Creating and Serving Profitable Customers," *California Management Review*, 43 (Summer), 118-142.

Building Consumer
Relationships Electronically

Shelby H. McIntyre

Santa Clara University

SUMMARY. This article addresses a set of interrelated issues in electronic Consumer Relationship Management (eCRM). The focus is specifically on an e-tailing context which consists of (a) consumers purchasing search goods of medium price, that (b) are delivered physically. The discussion deals with: (1) the relational needs of *online* consumers; (2) whose relational commitment emerges from a staged process; (3) involving an accumulated series of satisfying transactions; (4) that may entail different transaction types; and (5) with satisfaction on any given occasion being based on achievement relative to their expectations. These five components form a framework for building the eCRM business. The archetype for this e-tailing format is Amazon.com which, therefore, is used as a running example. *[Article copies available for a fee from The Haworth Document Delivery Service: 1-800-HAWORTH. E-mail address: <docdelivery@haworthpress.com> Website: <http://www.HaworthPress. com>* © 2003 by The Haworth Press, Inc. All rights reserved.]

Shelby H. McIntyre is Professor of Marketing, Marketing Department, Santa Clara University, Santa Clara, CA 95053 (E-mail: smcintyre@scu.edu).

The author is grateful for the contributions of Thomas Burnham, Larisa Genins, Kirthi Kalyanam, Subom Rhee, Max Sutherland, and particularly Tyzoon Tyebjee, along with that of the anonymous reviewers.

[Haworth co-indexing entry note]: "Building Consumer Relationships Electronically." McIntyre, Shelby H. Co-published simultaneously in *Journal of Relationship Marketing* (Best Business Books, an imprint of The Haworth Press, Inc.) Vol. 2, No. 3/4, 2003, pp. 15-30; and: *Customer Relationship Management in Electronic Markets* (ed: Gopalkrishnan R. Iyer, and David Bejou) Best Business Books, an imprint of The Haworth Press, Inc., 2003, pp. 15-30. Single or multiple copies of this article are available for a fee from The Haworth Document Delivery Service [1-800-HAWORTH, 9:00 a.m. - 5:00 p.m. (EST). E-mail address: docdelivery@haworthpress.com].

Digital Object Identifier: 10.1300/J366v02n03_02

KEYWORDS. Relationship marketing, trust, commitment, retailing, e-tailing, online shopping

In order to better practice Customer Relationship Management (CRM) in online consumer markets, it is beneficial to understand why the consumer would desire an electronic relationship and, therefore, how this desire might best be enhanced. Sheth and Parvatiyar (1995) have posited a number of factors that cause consumers, in general, to want a relationship with a given provider and Bendapudi and Berry (1997) have investigated the consumer's relationship motivations with respect to *service* providers. Marketers also want such a relationship, it being less costly to transact with a returning customer than to woo a new one (Blattberg and Deighton 1996; Day, 2000; Mckenna, 1991; Peters, 1988; Reichheld, 1993; 1994; 1996). The Web offers a new medium for achieving such relationships in an automated and, therefore, cost efficient way (Gruen, 1997). Amazon.com is considered to be a leading player in this online e-tailing arena and it becomes the natural benchmark against which to study Consumer Relationship Management online.

The rapidly accumulating literature on customer relationship management has its beginnings in a business-to-business context (Ford, 1990; Hallen, Johanson, and Seyed-Mohamed, 1991; Kalwani and Narayandas, 1995; Parasuraman, Berry, and Zeithaml, 1991; Sheth and Pavatiyar, 1993; Zeithaml, Berry, and Parasuraman, 1993). More recently a business-to-consumer focus has emerged (Sirdeshmukh, Singh, and Sabol, 2002). Both services (Lemon, Barnett White and Winer, 2002) and retailing (Cross and Smith, 1994; Gattuso, 1994; Gill, 1991; Reynolds and Beatty, 1999; Zimmerman 1992) have been addressed. However, less research has dealt with the topic of *electronic Consumer Relationship Management* (eCRM[1]), although the term is common in the trade press and actually constitutes a small but rapidly growing industry of service and software providers (Anton and Petouhoff, 1996; Greenspan, 2002).

On the academic side, there have been empirical studies about building trust online (Dayal, Landesberg, and Zeisser, 2000), the use of online shopping aids (Liechty, Ramaswamy and Cohen 2001), a model of online pre-purchase intentions (Shim, Eastlick, Lotz and Warrington 2001), and even a lab study about gaining intimate information via computer (Moon, 2000). Another study addressed the issue of service retention in regard to an online video-game service and the importance of the consumer's anticipation of future usage patterns (Lemon, Barnett White, and Winer, 2002). However, the existing academic consumer-oriented CRM work has yet to provide an integrated treatment of several important and interrelated topics including: (1) *the relational needs of* online *consumers*, (2) whose relational *commitment emerges from a staged process*, (3) involving an *accumulated series of satisfying transactions* (4) that may entail *different transaction types*, with (5) satisfaction on any given occasion being based largely on *achievement relative to expectations*.

This article addresses these interrelated issues in electronic Consumer Relationship Management (eCRM) and focuses specifically on an e-tailing context which is (a) for consumers purchasing search goods of medium price, that (b) are delivered physically. The archetype for this e-tailing format is Amazon.com which is an undisputed leader in this field and is, therefore, used as a running example.[2]

There are a truly vast number of ways in which Amazon.com builds a relationship with its customers. Because of the fact that the company is solely on-line, every transaction is automatically a database record. These records then become the foundation of everything that Amazon.com does and is an integral foundation for the entire electronic Customer Relationship Management (eCRM) process. Amazon.com has introduced over 40 relationship-management features on its web-site. These fall into the broad categories of notification services, recommendation services, community services, gift registry services and vendor services. For instance, one widely known relationship feature is the 1-click ordering process, which received a business process patent from the U.S. patent office in 1999. Collaborative filtering and reviews of books by users are some examples of recommendations services. E-mail shipment notification and back order management are examples of notification services. One could almost view the entire Amazon enterprise as an automated Customer Relationship building machine.

THE RELATIONAL NEEDS OF ONLINE CONSUMERS

Consumers, first of all, want a satisfactory experience in every transaction. They tend to understand, both intuitively and through experience, that repeated purchases from the same source (a) saves time, and (b) reduces risk (Bendapudi and Berry, 1997). Also, consumers want to avoid switching costs (Keaveney, 1995) which recently have been categorized into (a) time and effort costs, (b) financial costs, and (c) emotional costs of switching (Burnham, Frels and Mahajan, 2002). Consumers may even believe intuitively that being a loyal customer will lead to better treatment because of that loyalty (Dick and Basu 1994). However, to counter all of these "stickiness" forces, competing marketers are always offering incentives to induce switching. Thus, there is actually continual competition for a current relationship against other possible alternative ones (McGahan and Ghemawat, 1994).

However, consumers have additional specific desires to be relational when they are transacting online. First of all, there is the fact that many web-sites place cookies (e.g., tracking devices) on the user's machine and consumers have security fears about these cookies. By frequenting fewer providers there is less exposure to cookies and spam e-mail. Also this allows the returning consumer to (a) be recognized by the site, (b) have content personalized to them, and (c) allow login and other site privileges to be automatic. However, it is controversial as to how much of a benefit consumers actually perceive to come from personalization (Nunes and Kambil, 2001). Also, consumers have security concerns about the exposure of their credit card(s) online, and therefore want to give out this information sparingly, resulting in a desire to deal with as few sites as possible. Furthermore, there is the issue of learning about how to use a site: its look-and-feel, where to find particular features, etc. It takes time and effort to learn the subtleties of each site and, therefore, returning to a familiar one has an advantage over exploring a new one in terms of time and effort. Another factor is the constant bombardment by the popular press of the fact that there is fraud on the Internet and that the risks of using unknown suppliers is quite real. This leads to relying on the better-known suppliers (a relational issue) and returning to those who have performed well in the past.

Relationships require not only recognizing the relational needs of customers, but also acknowledging what they do not want thrust upon them (Fournier, Dobscha and Mick, 1998). In today's world of eCRM, the typical on-line consumer is bombarded with far more vendor relationships than their bandwidth can accommodate. It is critical to understand that ultimately it is Amazon's customer who chooses to have a relationship with Amazon. The relationship is built on not just having the customer's book needs served, but also his/her need for trust and respect served. Amazon is careful to respect privacy needs, provide security in transactions, and not spam its customer base. Every communication and touch point is instigated only to the extent that it adds value, which means that Amazon must create systems which allow it to understand customers at the individual level.

COMMITMENT EMERGES FROM A STAGED PROCESS

A consumer probably does not start off with the intention of establishing a long-term relationship with an online book supplier. Rather, the commitment to Amazon.com, for instance, comes from a staged process (Beatty, Mayer, Coleman, Reynolds and Lee, 1996; Gunlach, Achrol, and Mentzer, 1995). First, the consumer learns about the company from the popular press, friends and relatives, and possibly online sources. This leads to a visit to the site. Given confidence, based on these communications, the consumer may purchase a first book, thinking of it as a risky trial. The Amazon.com site provides several steps of positive reinforcement for the worried first-time consumer. First, there is an almost immediate e-mail acknowledging receipt of the order. This acknowledgement is very reassuring of the fact that the transaction is starting off well. Then, within a few hours or days a second e-mail informs the consumer that the item has been shipped. This provides further reinforcement that things are moving along in the transaction. Finally, the item arrives in the mail completing the transaction and providing affirmation of the consumer's choice to shop at Amazon.com. Still later, the consumer's credit card statement arrives and the consumer can verify that the transaction was billed at the correct amount. This successful round of information about the transaction establishes a feeling of trust in Amazon.com on the part of the consumer and hence lowers perceived risk for a future transaction. This trust then leads to further purchases. The essential point is that relationships are built and reinforced by "touch points." By building in a wide range of "touch points" into a single purchase transaction, Amazon creates the opportunity to remind customers of the relationship and, in the case of first time customers, to surprise them with information that they are not expecting but learn to appreciate. Additionally, Amazon is training its customers in how to interact with Amazon. By pre-empting queries that customers may have, Amazon reduces its cost-to-serve returning customers.

As the trust level in Amazon.com's reliability builds and its perceived risk diminishes, the consumer may commit to further efficiency of time and effort by turning on the 1-click settings at Amazon.com in order to speed the checkout process. This, of course, leads to further relational benefits. Also, the consumer may investigate her account and learn that there is an historical list of all the books that she has purchased, when, and at what price. If book shopping is done at more than this one site, the benefit of a full history of online book purchases is diluted leading to yet another relational benefit to staying with Amazon.com. At some point, the consumer may decide to use Amazon.com for the purchase of a gift that will be sent across the country to a recipient (possibly a niece in Baltimore). In this case, the consumer will enter the address and other information about that recipient. The book will be shipped. Thereafter, the consumer can send additional items to that recipient without re-entering the shipping address and contact information, leading to yet more efficiency for the consumer. Once again, Amazon has generated marketing efficiencies for itself. Not only is the sender part of a staged relationship process, the gift recipient also becomes the target for relationship building. The gift recipient becomes a member of Amazon's community and, hence its database, receiving transaction-specific messages as well as promotional messages. In effect, Amazon's customer acquisition costs are reduced.

Meanwhile, the Amazon.com website is learning about the interests of the returning consumer and is adjusting its collaborative filtering and recommendation engines based on the observed interests of that consumer. Thus, there is a joint learning cycle that is going on and the result is better recommendations, more efficiency in the transactions, less risk on both sides of the relationship, and growing trust and commitment by the consumer (Peppers and Rogers, 1999; Morgan and Hunt 1994). So, what started off as a trial purchase can end up in a long-term commitment, but it is built on one transaction after another in a staged process, rather than it being a pre-conceived desire by the consumer for such a relationship from the outset.

ACCUMULATED SERIES OF SATISFYING TRANSACTIONS

As noted, trust and commitment are built on a foundation of successful exchanges which reduce risk and increase efficiency. Only by repeated transactions can the consumer gain the experience needed to determine the true reliability and riskiness of the provider. Without the experience, a degree of skepticism is likely to linger. However, it is not necessarily the end of the road when a particular transaction goes astray. For instance, if Amazon.com delivers the wrong title to the consumer, the next issue is the attribution that the consumer will make about the error (Folkes, 1998). Does the consumer attribute the error to her having actually ordered improperly? Does she come to realize that there are two books with the same title? Is the failure attributed to a random, but perceived to be very infrequent, actual error on the part of Amazon.com? Learning theory tells us that *partial* reinforcement can still lead to substantial learning that is actually more resistant to forgetting and extinction than in the case of perfect positive reinforcement (Shimp, Stuart, and Engle, 1991). The next issue is what Amazon.com does about that bad outcome for the consumer. Sometimes such a so-called "service failure" can become an opportunity to show the exasperated consumer that the company stands behind its promises (Keaveney, 1995; Bitner, 1995). Until such an encounter, the customer never really knows how committed the provider is with respect to guaranteeing satisfaction on every transaction. The fact of the matter is that in the early days of its existence, Amazon.com had a good deal of problems achieving accurate shipments because it was simply passing on orders to publishers who were then in charge of the box-pack-and-ship operation. But few publishers were capable of making reliable, timely one-at-a-time shipments to consumers. The fact that Amazon.com finally built its own warehouses and took over the entire box-pack-and-ship operation proved the company's commitment to the customer (Bezos, 2000).

The box-pack-and-ship operation is only one element of the value chain which can contribute to a service failure. In this case, Amazon.com chose to take control of this element of the value chain by investing in the warehouses and pick-and-pack systems. In other critical elements of the value chain, it chooses to partner with other companies. For example, for the logistics function of delivering books to the doorstep of the consumer, Amazon.com relies on a partner courier service. The partner is of course chosen to guarantee the service level promised by Amazon.com. A more subtle point is that this partner now becomes part of the relationship building process. Information systems tie Amazon.com to its partners so that the customer can get from Amazon.com information, such as shipping status, that in fact resides with the partner. Complaints about delivery can go directly to Amazon.com who will then communicate these to the partner. Amazon.com is thereby able to control the entire relationship with its customers rather than allow it to be dispersed across several members of the value chain (publishers, couriers, payment systems, etc.).

DIFFERENT TRANSACTION TYPES

One of the most important aspects of maintaining and deepening a customer relationship is to satisfy that customer on each occasion. However, the same customer is very likely to have different shopping needs on different occasions (Keaveney 1995; Seybold, 2001). In one case, the shopper may learn of a specific book title from a friend and simply want to find and purchase that one item as quickly and conveniently as possible. On another occasion, the shopper my be interested in a general topic and want to know of any books that relate to that specific topic. At Christmas time, the shopper may be mostly motivated by the desire to use Amazon.com as a multi-location shipment delivery service which can provide large time and effort conveniences to someone with a long list of gift recipients. Thus, the buyer's need might result in different transaction types. Table 1 lists some of the most frequent and important transaction types at Amazon.com.

While it is one thing to recognize that serving these many needs are opportunities for Amazon to satisfy its customers, it is quite another thing to invite customers to utilize the services that Amazon.com offers. Amazon.com facilitates this by designing a website which is easy to navigate and focuses on each of these needs as a "use scenario." As customers go through various screens of the consideration and purchase process, information appears on a "just-in-time" basis so that the shopper is not burdened with information overload.

TABLE 1. Transaction Types

Transaction Type	Description
Item Need	The customer has learned about a specific book and simply wants to buy it as quickly and easily as possible.
Topic Need	The shopper wants to find a book about a given topic but is not sure which one.
Latent Need	The shopper desires a book, but is unaware of it without some prompting.
Opinion Need	The customer wants to know what other people have to say about a book he is considering.
Gift Giving Need	The shopper wants to give a book as a gift.
Gift Receiving Need	The shopper wants to receive a book as a gift (say for a birthday or wedding gift).
General Information Need	The shopper wants to know about books, but is not interested in buying anything.
Selling Need	The shopper has a book that he/she wants to sell.
Multi-Delivery Need	The shopper has special delivery needs, e.g., wants to buy a book but have it delivered to an alternative address.
Return Need	The shopper wants to return a book already purchased.
Problem Resolution Need	The shopper has a problem and is not sure what to do (for instance, received the wrong title, was billed more than expected).
Order Tracking Need	The shopper wants to know the status of an order, backorder, or forward order.

Given all of these transaction types, it is clear that service fulfillment is a complicated matter, and consumers are not liable to understand the difficulties behind different transactions. To them, it is all a matter of meeting expectations on each occasion, which brings us to the next point.

ACHIEVEMENT RELATIVE TO EXPECTATIONS

One of the ironies of achieving consumer satisfaction is that the yardstick used by the consumer is their expectations going into the transaction process. The expectations come about from several sources: (a) word-of-mouth from friends, (b) reading in the popular press, (c) experiences in other transactions both in general and possibly at competitors, (d) the promises made by the provider/site (Bitner 1995) and also (e) simple logic. With regard to the "communication" issue, consumers have a natural expectation that Amazon.com will have almost any book that they might want to purchase, it having been advertised as "the largest bookstore in the world." With regard to the "logic" issue, the very concept of a virtual bookstore suggests no shelf-space limitations. Also, there is a certain "logic" that suggests books should be less expensive at Amazon.com, it being online and, therefore, seeming to have a less costly business to operate compared to a large store-based book operation. Amazon maintains a network of book brokers who may supply the book. This network is transparent to the customer who may elect to have a particular broker supply the book. In this manner, Amazon leverages other vendors in living up to the promise of being the largest bookstore. Also, the brokers may offer books at different prices and customers are thereby offered the opportunity to comparison shop for price. This reinforces the customer's perception that they have the opportunity to receive the book at the lowest possible price. Additionally, many shoppers know that Amazon.com, as with many mail-order operations, does not charge sales tax (a point that has received much popular press attention). Therefore, the impression is likely to materialize that books at Amazon.com will be priced at least as cheaply as at local bookstores. However, these very expectations then set a high hurdle for Amazon.com against which it is necessary to achieve positive outcomes. It is this cycle of building expectations and living up to promises which is the key ingredient of eCRM.

BUILDING THE ECRM BUSINESS

What lessons can be learned from Amazon's success at building a eCRM business? A five-step process can help replicate Amazon's best practices into other consumer on-line businesses (see Figure 1). These are:

1. Build the Customer Database

For the online marketer, the customer database is much more than a contact sheet with names, addresses, and some key demographics. In-

FIGURE 1. Building the eCRM Business

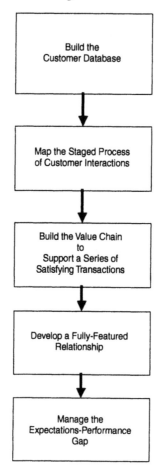

stead, the customer database is best viewed as a relationship diary in which the company records all its experiences with a customer. This database must capture the textual richness of these experiences. Relationships, unlike transaction, embrace a variety of interactions such as visiting, browsing, searching, purchasing, etc. This database becomes a relationship-building tool going beyond being a mere record of a customer's behavior. When there is a built-in capability to infer future needs from the trail of past behavior, the power of eCRM is unleashed. What John is likely to read in the future, based on what we know he has considered, evaluated and purchased in the past, is the question that needs to be answered. This requires the vendor to understand the merchandising relationships within its product line, which in turn can be better understood by examining the baskets of products that are purchased across the entire database, as well as the inherent technical/topical relationships within the product line.

2. Map the Staged Process of Customer Interactions

Every purchase transaction can be mapped into a series of activities performed by the customer and the vendor. As the order fulfillment process moves through these stages, the vendor can increase the transparency of this staged process by providing information to the customer. As a series of messages to the customer are generated over this staged process, the relationship is enhanced in three ways. First, the resulting transparency of the process demonstrates respect for the customer's right to remain informed. Second, the customer feels a sense of control over aspects of the transaction which are, in actuality, entirely in the hands of the vendor. Third, each stage-specific message to the customer is a "touch point" which reinforces the relationship.

3. Build The Value Chain to Support a Series of Satisfying Transactions

Service failures put the relationship at risk. The value chain which supports an online vendor can typically be parsed into four major components: (a) the IT infrastructure which hosts the web interface and services to the customer, (b) the fulfillment infrastructure which sources, warehouses, sorts and assorts products, (c) the logistics infrastructure which delivers products to the customer, and (d) the payment infrastructure which manages the flow of funds between customers and the vendor. At its very extreme, a virtual online vendor is entirely a marketing organization with the IT, fulfillment, logistics and payment services hosted at partner organizations. In reality, every online vendor must wrestle with the "make vs. buy" decision around these four infrastructures. This decision must of course weigh the investment needed to build such an infrastructure. From, an eCRM point of view, the decision requires the additional consideration of the risk of service failure if the vendor does not control certain elements of the infrastructure. Once'the decision is made to partner for aspects of the infrastructure, a strong partner management program needs to be put into place to guarantee each consumer a series of satisfying transactions.

4. Build a Fully-Featured Relationship

The richness of a relationship can be gauged in terms of the range of needs that it serves. One way on-line vendors can broaden their engagement with customers is by widening their product offering. For example, though this paper has described Amazon mostly as a book e-tailer, Amazon today offers toys, computer software, entertainment software, and electronics. Another way to broaden the engagement is to cater to a variety of information needs of customers within a particular product category. A typology of these information needs was provided in Table 1. Thus an on-line vendor must view its business as both product offerings and information service offerings at the same time.

5. Manage the Expectations-Performance Gap

Customer satisfaction is a result of the experience of customers with the performance of a vendor calibrated against their expectations of how that vendor will perform. The previous four steps of building the eCRM business have been concerned with improving the vendor's performance and enhancing the customer's experience. Equally important is to manage customer expectations which act to establish the base line against which the vendor's performance is judged. The relatively virgin territory of online marketing has resulted in a "land grab" mentality where vendors are more concerned with customer acquisition (even only their eyeballs will do) than with customer satisfaction and retention. This has resulted in a substantial amount of hype in promoting to customers. The philosophy of eCRM is to calibrate promises to customers against the actual ability of the online business' ability to deliver against these promises. The practical reality of this philosophy is to put in place a dashboard of service level metrics. These metrics then serve the dual purpose of driving service level improvement as well as messaging promises to customers.

CONCLUSION

Overall, if we are willing to generalize from the Amazon.com example and the benchmark it provides, it is clear that electronic Consumer Relationship Management has several advantages. First of all, it is a natural extension of the principle that allowing the customer to apply self-service in an automated way can accomplish great supply-side efficiencies. When the result also comes across to the consumer as better service, a win-win situation has been achieved (Kelley, Donnelly, and Skinner, 1990). This is the result that occurred in the early 1920s, when the telephone companies originally eliminated telephone operators on all calls and instead allowed consumers to dial their own numbers; huge supply-side efficiencies ensued and consumers felt better served in the end. Similarly, when the old general store with the clerk who took the customer's order and brought the goods to the counter was replaced by the then novel supermarket format, huge supply-side efficiencies were achieved and consumers felt better served even though they performed most of the work. Now we arrive at the online bookstore, and again automation stands to achieve large supply-side efficiencies while consumers perceive the result as better service. Thus, the foundation of electronic Customer Relationship Management is better service through supply-side automation. But the model depends upon the marketing and relationship management side of the equation. As has been pointed out herein, the service provider must (a) anticipate the consumers relational needs; (b) nurture the consumer's commitment as it emerges from a staged process; (c) involving an accumulated series of transactions; (d) of different transaction types; and (e) all with achievement being measured against the consumer's expectations as the yardstick. This analysis of the relationship building process suggests the core considerations for building the eCRM business starts with building the customer database. Next, it is important to map the staged process of customer interactions as a key to an effective site-design, incorporating the appropriate "use scenarios" for all the important transaction types that are liable to occur. That user-based design then indicates how to build the value chain needed to support it. Finally, customer communication can help to manage the expectations-performance gap to minimize service failures and the negative perceptions they produce.

NOTES

1. Winer, Russell S. (2001), "A Framework for Customer Relationship Management," *California Management Review*, Vol 42, No. 4, (Summer), 2001 points out that: "If all the components of the CRM system are Web-based, including the company, eCRM (electronic CRM) is sometimes the term that is used."

2. For simplicity of exposition, the focus of attention in these examples is on the book division of Amazon.com

REFERENCES

Anton, Jon, and Natalie L. Petouhoff (1996), *Customer Relationship Management*, Pearson Education, Upper Saddle River: New Jersey.

Beatty, Sharon E., Morris Mayer, James Coleman, Kristy Ellis Reynolds, and Jungki Lee (1996), "Customer-Sales Associate Retail Relationships," *Journal of Retailing*, 72 (3), 223-247

Bendapudi, Neeli, and Leonard L. Berry, (1997), "Customers' Motivations for Maintaining Relationships with Service Providers," *Journal of Retailing*, 73 (Spring), 15-37

Bezos, J. (2000), Keynote Speech at Harvard Business School Cyberposium, 26 Feb. 2000

Bitner, Mary Jo (1995), "Building Service Relationships: It's All About Promises (Comment on Berry)," *Journal of the Academy of Marketing Science*, Vol. 23, (Fall), 246-51

Blattberg, Robert C., and John Deighton (1996), "Managing Marketing by the Customer Equity Test," *Harvard Business Review*, 74 (July-August), 136-144

Burnham, Thomas A., Judy K. Frels, and Vijay Mahajan (2002), "The Antecedents and Consequences of Consumer Switching Costs," *Journal of the Academy of Marketing Science*, (forthcoming)

Cross, Richard, and Janet Smith (1994), "Retailers Move Toward New Customer Relations," *Direct Marketing*, Vol. 57 (December), 20-22

Day, George (2000), "Managing Marketing Relationships," *Journal of the Academy of Marketing Science*, 28 (Winter), 24-30

Dayal, Sandeep, Helene Landesberg, and Michael Zeisser (2000), "How to Build Trust Online," *Marketing* Management, (Fall), 64-69

Dick, Alan S. and Kunal Basu (1994), "Customer Loyalty. Toward An Integrated Conceptual Framework," *Journal of the Academy of Marketing Science*, Vol. 22 (Spring), 99-113

Folkes, Valerie S. (1998), "Recent Attribution Research in Consumer Behavior: A Review and New Directions," *Journal of Consumer Research*, 14 (4), 548-565

Ford, David (1990), *Understanding Business Markets, Interaction, Relationships, and Networks*, London: Academic Press

Fournier, Susan, Susan Dobscha, and David Mick (1998), "Preventing The Premature Death of Relationship Marketing," *Harvard Business Review*, 76 (January-February), 42-51

Gattuso, Gary (1994), "Relationship Retailing. A Two-Way Street," *Direct Marketing*, Vol. 56, (Feb), 38, 41

Gill, Penny (1991), "Added Value: Relationship Marketing Is One Way for Retailers to Build Loyalty," *Stores*, Vol. 73, (Oct), 39-40

Greenspan, Robyn (2002), "CRM Spending on the Upswing," *eCRM News*, April 9, 1-3

Gruen, Thomas W. (1997), "Relationship Marketing: The Route to Marketing Efficiency and Effectiveness," *Business Horizons*, 40 (November/December), 32-38

Gunlach, Gregory T., Ravi S. Achrol, and John T. Mentzer (1995), "The Structure of Commitment in Exchange," *Journal of Marketing*, 59 (1), 78-92

Hallen, Lars, Jan Johanson, and Nazeem Seyed-Mohamed (1991), "Interfirm Adaptation in Business Relationships," *Journal of Marketing*, 55 (2), 29-37

Kalwani, Manohar U., and Narakesari Narayandas (1995), "Long-Term Manufacturer-Supplier Relationships: Do They Pay Off for Supplier Firms?" *Journal of Marketing*, 59 (1), 1-16.

Keaveney, Susan M (1995), "Customer switching behavior in service industries. An exploratory study," *Journal of Marketing*, Vol. 59, (April), 71-82

Kelley, Scott W., James H. Donnelly, Jr., and Steven J. Skinner (1990), "Customer Participation in Service Production and Delivery," *Journal of Retailing*, 66 (3), 315-335

Lemon, Katherine N., Tiffany Barnett White, and Russell S. Winer (2002), "Dynamic Customer Relationship Management: Incorporating Future Considerations into the Service Retention Decision," *Journal of Marketing*, 66 (January), 1-14

Liechty, John, Venkatram Ramaswamy, and Steven H. Cohen (2001), *Journal of Marketing Research*, 38 (May), 183-196

McKenna, Regis (1991), *Relationship Marketing: Successful Strategies for the Age of the Customer*, Persues Books, New York: NY

McGahan, A.M., and Pankaj Ghemawat (1994), "Competition to Retain Customers," *Marketing Science*, 13 (Spring), 165-176

Moon, Youngme (2000), "Intimate Exchanges: Using Computers to Elicit Self-Disclosure from Consumers," *Journal of Consumer Research*, 26 (March), 323-39

Morgan, Robert M, Hunt, Shelby D. (1994), "The Commitment-Trust Theory of Relationship Marketing," *Journal of Marketing*, Vol. 58 (July), 20-38

Nunes, Paul F., and Ajit Kambil (2001), "Personalization? No Thanks," Forethought, Harvard Business School Publishing, Cambridge: MA

Parasuraman, A., Leonard L. Berry, and Valerie A. Zeithaml (1991), "Understanding Customer Expectations of Service," *Sloan Management Review*, 32 (Spring), 39-48

Peppers, Don, and Martha Rogers (1993), *The One to One Future*, New York, NY: Doubleday

Peppers, Don, and Martha Rogers (1997), *Enterprise One to One*, New York, NY: Doubleday

Peppers, Don and Martha Rogers (1999a), *The One to One Manager*, New York, NY: Doubleday

Peppers, Don and Martha Rogers (1999b), *The One to One Fieldbook*, New York, NY: Doubleday

Peters, Thomas (1988), *Thriving on Chaos*, New York: Harper and Row

Reichheld, Frederick F. (1994), "Loyalty and the Renaissance of Marketing," *Marketing Management*, Vo. 2, No. 4, 10-21

Reichheld, Frederick F. (1996), *The Loyalty Effect*, Cambridge, MA: Harvard Business School Press

Reichheld, Frederick F., (1993), "Loyalty-Based Management," *Harvard Business Review*, Vol. 71, (March/April), 64-73

Reynolds, Kristy E., and Sharon E. Beatty (1999), "A Relationship Customer Typology," *Journal of Retailing*, 75 (Winter), 509-23

Rogers, Martha, and Don Peppers (1994b), "Relationship Marketing: Planning for Share of Customer, Not Market Share," in *Relationship Marketing: Theory, Methods and Applications*, ed. Jagdish N. Sheth, Atul Parvatiyar, Center for Relationship Marketing, Roberto C. Goizueta Business School, Emory University

Seybold, Patricia (2001), "Get Inside the Lives of Your Customers," *Harvard Business Review*, (May), 81-89

Sheth, Jagdish N. and Atul Parvatiyar (1993), "The Evolution of Relationship Marketing," Presented at the Sixth Conference on Historical Thought in Marketing, Atlanta

Sheth, Jagdish N. and Atul Parvatiyar (1995), "Relationship Marketing in Consumer Markets: Antecedents and Consequences," *Journal of the Academy of Marketing Science*, Vol. 23, (Fall), 255-71

Shim, Soyeon, Mary Ann Eastlick, Sherry L. Lotz, and Patricia Warrington (2001), "An Online Prepurchase Intentions Model: The Role of Intention to Search," *Journal of Retailing*, 77, 39-416

Shimp, Terence A., Elnora W. Stuart, and Randall W. Engle (1991), "A Program of Classical Conditioning Experiments Testing Variations in the Conditioned Stimulus and Context," *Journal of Consumer Research*, 18 (1), 1-12

Sirdeshmukh, Deepak, Jagdip Singh, and Barry Sabol (2002), "Consumer Trust, Value, and Loyalty in Relational Exchanges," *Journal of Marketing*, 66 (January), 15-37

Winer, Russell S. (2001), "A Framework for Customer Relationship Management," *California Management Review*, 43 (Summer), 89-105

Zeithaml, Valerie A., Leonard L. Berry, and A. Parasuraman (1993), "The Nature and Determinants of Customer Expectations of Service," *Journal of the Academy of Marketing Science*, 21 (Winter), 1-12

Zimmerman, Raymond (1992), "Relationship Marketing," *Retail Business Review*, Vol. 60, 8, 4-8

Loyalty in e-Tailing:
A Conceptual Framework

Dhruv Grewal
Babson College

Joan Lindsey-Mullikin
Babson College

Jeanne Munger
University of Southern Maine

SUMMARY. Internet retailers that attempt to establish a steady customer base by offering the lowest price are not basing their expectations on firm ground. An alternative to low-price strategies is to develop and maintain a loyal customer base. In this paper, we present a framework for developing loyalty via the Internet. Internet strategies should be developed based upon the firm's competencies and an analysis of the current loyal customer base. The components of the Internet exchange–such as

Dhruv Grewal is the Toyota Chair of Commerce and Electronic Business, Babson College, Babson Park, MA 02457 (E-mail: dgrewal@babson.edu).

Joan Lindsey-Mullikin is Assistant Professor, Babson College, Babson Park, MA 02457 (E-mail: jmullikin@babson.edu).

Jeanne Munger is Assistant Professor, University of Southern Maine, Box 9300, Portland, ME 04104 (E-mail: jmunger@usm.maine.edu).

The authors' names are listed alphabetically.

[Haworth co-indexing entry note]: "Loyalty in e-Tailing: A Conceptual Framework." Grewal, Dhruv, Joan Lindsey-Mullikin, and Jeanne Munger. Co-published simultaneously in *Journal of Relationship Marketing* (Best Business Books, an imprint of The Haworth Press, Inc.) Vol. 2, No. 3/4, 2003, pp. 31-49; and: *Customer Relationship Management in Electronic Markets* (ed: Gopalkrishnan R. Iyer, and David Bejou) Best Business Books, an imprint of The Haworth Press, Inc., 2003, pp. 31-49. Single or multiple copies of this article are available for a fee from The Haworth Document Delivery Service [1-800-HAWORTH, 9:00 a.m. - 5:00 p.m. (EST). E-mail address: docdelivery@haworthpress.com].

31

site content, design, navigation and interactivity–are linked to convenience and risk perceptions. These in turn affect the satisfaction/loyalty and performance. Continuous evaluation of customers' perceptions of value determines the adjustments that need to be made to the existing retention activities. The benefits of Internet loyalty are discussed, along with directions for future research. *[Article copies available for a fee from The Haworth Document Delivery Service: 1-800-HAWORTH. E-mail address: <docdelivery@haworthpress.com> Website: <http://www.HaworthPress.com> © 2003 by The Haworth Press, Inc. All rights reserved.]*

KEYWORDS. Loyalty, e-loyalty, internet retailers, retailing, customer retention

INTRODUCTION

A fundamental goal for all retailers and service providers is to develop loyal customers. Past research has demonstrated that loyalty results in continued purchases, an increase in future purchases, and positive word of mouth (Sirohi, McLaughlin and Wittink 1998). Two fundamental and complementary strategies to achieve the revenue and profit that loyalty yields are to acquire new customers and retain existing ones.

A number of Internet retailers have attempted to focus on the first strategy–acquiring new customers–by offering lower prices. But on the Internet, price searches can be done with relative ease (e.g., *www. bizrate.com* and *www.mysimon.com*), and a firm's competitors can easily offer a more competitive pricing scheme, thus taking price sensitive customers away. Firms that cater to price sensitive customers are in fact predicted to have a dismal future (Reichheld and Schefter 2000) and often experience failure with pricing strategies aimed at acquiring new customers (Reichheld 1993). An alternative to low-price strategies is developing relationships with customers and creating a loyal customer base–a retention-oriented strategy.

The earlier emphasis on consumer acquisition was somewhat misplaced, the major issue today for e-tailers is how to provide the best value to the customer and solicit their loyalty. The Internet has provided marketers with an amazing opportunity to increase touch points with customers and ultimately enhance satisfaction and loyalty. Research has demonstrated that second-time website users spend on average twice the amount of money that first-time users do (Nielsen 1997). Furthermore, on-line customers exhibit a proclivity toward loyalty (Reichheld and Schefter 2000). Thus, the Internet can greatly facilitate relationship building/retention strategies.

In this paper, we have explicitly tried to limit our focus to the use of the Internet by incumbent retailers that have traditionally been brick and mortar (J.C. Penney, Wal-Mart) or catalogue (Land's End, L.L. Bean, Dell). We feel that the past few years have not played out well for the pure clicks (Grewal, Iyer and Levy 2003). Thus, using the Internet in the current environment seems to favor traditional incumbents. These retailers have an established reputation (or brand equity) and do not have to invest millions of dollars in generating brand awareness as well as site awareness (e.g., *www.walmart.com* or *www.dell.com*).

According to a study by *Chain Store Age* (2001), 51% of online shoppers were first attracted to the merchandise via a catalogue. For example, customers might look over a catalogue for ideas and shop online for more specific product information. The availability of multiple channels has an added benefit–multiple-channel customers often spend more than single-channel customers. Store shoppers who visit a particular retailer's web site purchase more frequently and spend more than the average shopper. For example at J.C. Penney, customers who shop all three of its channels–store, catalogue and web–spent an average of $1,050 each in 1999, over four times the amount spent by shoppers who used one channel exclusively (Scheraga 2000).

In the next section we propose and discuss a conceptual framework that integrates the role of the Internet with the value-loyalty-profit paradigm. This framework builds on past research on technology and the Internet (Parasuraman and Grewal 2000; Montoya-Weiss, Voss and Grewal 2002) and links it to satisfaction/loyalty and profits (Heskett, Sasser, and Schlesinger 1997; Reichheld 1994).

CONCEPTUAL FRAMEWORK

Our framework has eight major components. The first two components highlight the need for managers to explicitly take into account their *goals* and their *customer base* (new and existing) in developing their strategies. We explicitly focus on their effects on *merchandise* and *Internet-factors* (e.g., content, design, navigation), which are our third and fourth model components. We then examine the role of merchandise and Internet factors on customers' value perceptions. Value is assessed in terms of two factors (5th and 6th model components):

convenience (to capture the benefit side of the equation) and *risk* (to capture the loss side of the equation). Finally, these convenience and risk perceptions are likely to affect the *satisfaction/loyalty* and in turn retailer *performance* (our final two model components). The basic components of these linkages are depicted in Figure 1.

FIRM GOALS AND COMPETENCIES

Goals are general statements of desired accomplishments expressed in qualitative terms (Ferrell, Hartline, Lucas and Luck 1998). They are important because they provide direction for the firm and help to create a set of priorities the firm will use in committing its resources (Ferrell, Hartline, Lucas and Luck 1998). Maintaining a presence on the Internet makes it increasingly necessary to carefully monitor goals and strategy and firms have to distinguish themselves through the strategies they use to achieve their goals (Porter 2001).

Marketing on the Internet can be broken down into three activities: transactions, distribution, and communication (Peterson, Balasubramanian and Bronnenberg 1997). A firm determines its Internet competencies within one or more of these and then must choose a target base of customers. Management can use the Internet to develop retention based goals for the specific segment (Reichheld 1993).

FIGURE 1. Internet-Based Loyalty Framework

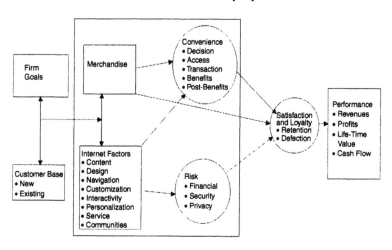

Retention as an Internet strategy is critical since competition is enormous and constantly acquiring new customers is very expensive. Design elements of the Internet exchange–site design, convenience, financial security, and merchandise (Szymanski and Hise 2000)–should accommodate the customer group that we are trying to retain. Once these design elements have been implemented, management should continuously evaluate customers' perceptions of value in order to make adjustments to the retention strategy.

Loyalty is particularly important since it is estimated that web businesses take at least two to three years to recoup their initial acquisition investment (Reichheld and Schefter 2000). Loyal customers cost less to maintain, and are thus a relatively more profitable source of revenue during those building years. Furthermore, on-line customers have exhibited a proclivity toward loyalty (Reichheld and Schefter 2000), thus offering the opportunity to capitalize on this potential venue.

UNDERSTANDING THE CUSTOMER BASE

A firm should determine which customers it can best serve given its unique set of competencies and merchandise to be offered. It must base this on an understanding of what it is particularly good at given its core competencies. It can determine the extent to which these customers represent a new segment or existing customers. A customer retention orientation focuses on the existing customer base. It is the existing customer base that has the highest likelihood of being the most satisfied and thus the most loyal customers. The return of such programs can be significant. A 5% increase in retention can lead to a 25% to 95% increase in profits (Reichheld and Schefter 2000).

Companies should determine their own goals and competencies (prior model component) and seek out customers that are compatible with these competencies. This knowledge can be gained through data mining techniques in two ways. First, data mining can identify loyal or profitable customers and their attributes. Second, it can detect problems with operations that may have affected loyal customers during their interactions with the firm.

Appropriate data mining activities (Iyer, Miyazaki, Grewal and Giordano 2002) while generating high customer retention also generates positive word of mouth, which is even more powerful online. Furthermore, new online customers acquired by word of mouth often use the person that referred them for assistance, advice, and guidance in making their purchases, thus, saving firms per customer transaction costs.

MERCHANDISE

Retailers have to systematically and continually evaluate their goals and competencies and the needs of their customers in order to make appropriate merchandising decisions. Merchandise management is one of the most important facets of retailing (Levy and Weitz 2001), and it should result from a systematic analysis. The Internet can help a traditional retailer present a greater number of SKUs via the Internet. For example, SKUs that were slow moving and expensive to keep in inventory at Staples stores are being systematically moved to *www.staples.com.*

Internet shoppers are likely to worry about lack of trial, lack of interpersonal trust and lack of instant gratification (Grewal, Iyer and Levy 2003). Some categories of Internet merchandise are more likely to generate a positive response than others (Grewal, Iyer and Levy 2003). For example, collectibles, books, music CDs, and videos are widely bought over the Internet from retailers (e.g., *www.amazon.com*) and auction sites (e.g., *www.ebay.com*). Other categories such as groceries (e.g., Streamline and Webvan) have not panned out (Lisanti 2001, Wingfield 2001).

A web presence can allow the marketer to experiment with product assortment, gathering information within a very short time and without jeopardizing the existing product offerings in a physical store. For example, REI determined that existing customers would also buy fitness and fly-fishing equipment and offered these products on the web within a ten-week timeframe, as opposed to the typical six-month period necessary for launching a product trial in physical stores.

In general, products that have a high digital component are more likely to be successful over the web, as are standardized and branded products that have a clear value proposition (Peterson, Balasubramanian, and Bronnenberg 1997). Over time, the sale of these products is likely to be enhanced as consumer usage and acceptance of search engines and shopping bots increase (e.g., *www.mysimon.com* and *www.bizrate.com*).

INTERNET FACTORS:
CLICK VERSUS BRICK ISSUES

Traditional retailers can use the Internet to develop a web presence and sell merchandise online, which we term click issues. Consideration of these Internet factors can help retailers better serve their current customer base, locate new customers, and move customers to the web for certain slow-moving merchandise and items that are expensive to inventory or difficult to store. Using the Internet within their stores can also help retailers' salespersons better serve the customers, termed brick issues.

Click Issues

Conventional literature in the domain of store atmospherics or environment has identified numerous factors that can either enable or inhibit shopping (Baker, Parasuraman, Grewal and Voss 2002; Baker, Grewal and Levy 1992; Baker, Grewal and Parasuraman 1994). Some of these that have relevance to the Internet are store design and ambiance. Other crucial but web-specific factors that can help the click side of the retail business include website content, design and graphics, navigation, interactivity, personalization and service (Montoya-Weiss, Voss and Grewal 2002).

Website Content. The *information content,* varying from the merchandise or services offered to testimonials of satisfied customers, helps communicate the key objective of the website (Montoya-Weiss, Voss and Grewal 2002). It is essential to keep a close eye on the match between this information content and customer needs in order to facilitate long-term customer satisfaction. Click-through studies can help marketers identify valuable content.

Website Design. The *design and graphic style* of the website are akin to the atmospherics of a bricks-and-mortar operation (Lohse and Spiller 1999). The more inviting they are, the more customers are likely to revisit the site. The graphics, however, should not detract from the site's primary objectives nor adversely affect site navigation.

Website Navigation. Navigation, the number of clicks needed to get into and through the site, is linked to the structure of the site content (Montoya-Weiss, Voss and Grewal 2002; Spiller and Lohse 1999). Navigational features can facilitate purchases, searches, queries, and other transactions. The speed at which consumers can navigate a site enhances their ability to shop.

Web-Based Customization. The Internet has brought the concept of *customization* to a new level: led by Dell, more and more web-based operations are allowing customers to create their own products (Winer 2001). A choiceboard, as Slywotsky (2000) calls it, lets customers determine the specific features they want from a list of available product attributes. Such customization is inexpensive and relatively easy for some product categories like information goods (Shapiro and Varian 1999).

New technologies further enhance the functionality of web sites. Land's End shoppers, for example, can provide some simple measurements to order a pair of custom-made chinos that will be delivered within two to three weeks (Merrick 2001). This experience combines a custom fit with the convenience of web shopping along with cost savings relative to what it would cost to have an item tailor-made.

Website Interactivity. A number of researchers have demonstrated the importance of the *interactivity* of the website (e.g., Novak, Hoffman and Yung 2000). Interactivity involves the ability of the consumer to interact with the website. Such interactivity is likely to increase attention and arousal and result in greater "stickiness."

At Lands' End, for example, consumers simply complete a short questionnaire noting their preference level for six pairs of outfits, along with their aversions to specific fabrics, colors and styles. A feature called My Personal Shopper (MPS) then sorts through more than 90,000 apparel options to immediately recommend the most suitable items based on the shopper's preferences. Land's End can also assist customers by providing live customer service (Merrick 2001).

Website Personalization. Recent innovations have enabled retailers to personalize the information consumers see on a particular website, particularly in the banking and financial arena (for example, *www.fidelity.com*). One level of personalization can be conducted through cookies and online profiling (Baker, Marn and Zawada 2001; Iyer, Miyazaki, Grewal and Giordano 2002). Through various online tracking methodologies the retailer can infer preferences and customize the site with them.

Web-Service Issues. Retailers can provide online service by using queries to which customers can respond or help lines they can contact (e.g., e-mail to *www.dell.com* for technical help). Winer (2001) has pointed out how web-based services such as LivePerson, HumanClick and netCustomer offer plug-in modules that provide live customer service from participating firms (akin to a call center).

Web-Based Communities. A number of retailers have started to aggressively use the web to create online communities. These communities are a network of customers exchanging product information and insights with one another (Winer 2001). REI.com creates a community for outdoor enthusiasts who interact through message boards, exchanging adventure stories, seeking insights about products, and posting photos from their own travels.

Brick Issues

Retailers use the Internet effectively within their stores, both in web kiosks and as a tool for assisting store personnel.

In-Store Web Kiosks. Customers and salespeople can find merchandise that is not carried in the store but is sold by the retailer on the Internet through the use of in-store kiosks. Staples, for example, has developed a method to increase the availability of merchandise and provide greater convenience for customers through its in-store kiosks. The kiosks provide access to 100,000 SKUs beyond the standard 9,000 available in its stores. It has increased the average order amount because customers pay for all items at once, regardless of whether they were purchased in-store or via the kiosk (Chain Store Age 2001).

The Internet and the In-Store Sales-force. Grewal, Levy and Marshall (2003) recently articulated a number of different ways in which the sales-force could enhance selling effectiveness via the Internet. Some of them include:

- Reducing time spent on order status queries by directing customers to check on special orders online.
- Accessing customer histories online, so as to be more adaptive and suggestive in their selling.
- Helping customers make a purchase via the kiosk for out of stock items.

PERCEIVED VALUE PROPOSITION

Building on work by Montoya-Weiss, Voss and Grewal (2002), we can link the effects of merchandise and Internet factors to the value proposition. Research has demonstrated that consumers cognitively trade off benefits against costs to determine their value perceptions (e.g., Dodds, Monroe and Grewal 1991; Grewal, Monroe and Krishnan 1998). In this paper, we have focused on the *convenience aspects to capture the benefit side* of the value equation and *the risks to capture the sacrifice side* of the value equation.

Creating Customer Convenience

One of the key reasons for using the Internet is convenience–it reduces the time and effort put forth by consumers (Berry, Seiders and Grewal 2002). They identify five critical elements where retailers and service providers need to focus their efforts to enhance convenience. These are: decision convenience, access convenience, transaction convenience, benefits convenience and post-benefit convenience. Clearly, for the development of long-term loyalty, Internet retailers and service providers need to ensure that their sites address these convenience dimensions.

Decision Convenience. To enhance decision convenience, firms can provide appropriate information on their sites pertaining to the product, price and warranty. The development of a web presence was a natural extension of Recreational Equipment Incorporated's (REI) corporate goal to deliver any product, any time, any place and to answer any question. Through its web site, REI offers a broad selection of products, 24/7/365, throughout the world, while also providing the rich information necessary for selling its technological products.

Access Convenience. Firms can improve access by ensuring their sites are prominently displayed on various search engines (e.g., *www.yahoo.com* and *www.google.com*) and are easy to load. Customer interactions can be coordinated into one seamless operation. REI, for example, links its point-of-sale terminals to the Internet so cashiers can conduct product searches for customers. Even its smallest stores can make available the assortment of the largest store. Consumers can also remotely access *www.rei.com* for added convenience.

Purchase Convenience. Purchase transactions can be performed on the Internet in their entirety, saving time and money for both firm and customers. Readily available information also helps customers place accurate orders, increasing purchase convenience. Research, however, has found that over 60% of Internet shoppers abandon their web-carts before buying (Tedeschi 2000); a key reason is the slowness of the site (Cimino 2000). Thus, speed and ease of use are critical factors for completing the sale.

A number of Internet retailers require the customer to sign in (e.g., *www.e-bay.com* and *www.amazon.com*), a technique that maintains each user's purchase history and other relevant information and enhances the transactional convenience of a given site. Today most banks and financial institutions provide personalized pages that maintain similar records and make it easy to find account information and conduct transactions (see *www.fidelity.com*).

Benefit Convenience. Benefit convenience has been defined as the "consumers' perceived time and effort expenditures to experience the service's core benefits" (Berry, Seiders, and Grewal 2002). It is crucial for firms to help consumers efficiently and effectively get to the benefit stage and enjoy the benefits of the product or service that they are acquiring. Retailers and service providers of digital products can maximize benefit convenience with web-based delivery (or downloads) of information content (e.g., Wall Street Journal: *www.wsj.com*), financial reports (*www.fidleity.com*), software (*www.turbotax.com*) and music (Grewal, Iyer and Levy 2003).

Post-Benefit Convenience. The Internet is also a phenomenal tool for providing post-benefit convenience-dealing with product problems. For example, *www.dell.com* provides customer support and technical support pertaining to problems with Dell hardware. An online e-mail query to Dell will get a response in a relatively short time.

Reducing Risk Perceptions

Internet consumers are exposed to various levels of risk including security, financial, fulfillment, performance, and privacy risk (e.g., Grewal, Gotlieb and Marmorstein 1994; Grewal, Munger, Iyer and Levy 2003; Montoya-Weiss, Voss and Grewal 2002). Financial, security and privacy risks are likely to be of tantamount importance (Goldman Sachs Investment Research 2000).

Shopping on the Internet requires the provision of personal information (e.g., name, address and credit card) that takes away the anonymity of the shopper (Bhatnagar, Misra and Rao 2000). Consequently, consumers are likely to be concerned about their credit card information (financial and security risks) and the possible widespread use of personal information (privacy risks) (Goodwin 1991; Novak, Hoffman and Peralta 1999; Wang, Lee and Wang 1998).

Recent research suggests that key to enhancing consumer confidence and reducing their risk perceptions are factors such as store reputation, money-back guarantees and explicit provision of security information (Grewal, Munger, Iyer and Levy 2003). One way to do this is to avoid spam. Another is to use the Internet as an informational tool. For example, Vanguard's website just educates; its customers want to prevent access to their personal financial information, so the company avoids selling in order to build their trust (Reichheld and Schefter 2000).

The Relative Emphasis on Value

Because retailers develop customer relationships both to acquire new customers and to retain existing ones, they focus their efforts on enhancing both perceptions of value and customer satisfaction. Perceived value appears to play a profound role in the pre-purchase situation

(Dodds, Monroe and Grewal 1991, Grewal, Monroe and Krishnan 1998, Baker, Parasuraman, Grewal and Voss 2002) and it is likely to have a greater role if the firm's goal is customer acquisition. Satisfaction, however, appears to be critical in the post-purchase situation (Voss, Parasuraman and Grewal 1998). Consequently, if the goal is to develop relationships, loyalty and retention, we will clearly need to focus on satisfaction.

SATISFACTION AND LOYALTY

Jones and Sasser (1995) highlight the importance of perceived value in the quest for creating customer satisfaction and resulting loyalty: ". . . providing customers with outstanding value may be the only reliable way to achieve sustained customer satisfaction and loyalty" (p. 90). Research has emphasized that loyalty is earned by delivering *superior* value (Reichheld 1993) and that e-satisfaction leads to loyalty (Szymanski and Hise 2000).

While there has been increasing support for the contention that high levels of satisfaction drive loyalty, the relationship between these variables is also influenced by other factors. Jones and Sasser (1995) found the relationship between satisfaction and loyalty varies by industry. For example, in the automotive industry even a slight drop in satisfaction resulted in a large drop in loyalty. A similar finding was evidenced in the personal computer market, although it was less pronounced. In the airline industry and with hospitals, which are dominated by strong loyalty programs and high costs of switching, consumers are apt to exhibit loyalty across lower levels of satisfaction. Finally, in the local telephone market, which has nearly complete control over customers, users remained with their company regardless of their level of satisfaction or dissatisfaction. Individual firms must therefore understand the nature of the relationship between the firm's offering and its customers' satisfaction, value, and loyalty and then develop the metrics for its measurement.

PERFORMANCE CONSEQUENCES OF LOYALTY

Customer satisfaction is central to the notion of loyalty, and recent research indicates that increased levels of satisfaction can lead to improved financial performance. Anderson, Fornell and Lehmann (1994) found that increased levels of satisfaction yielded greater levels of loyalty and improved return on investment for manufacturing firms but found weaker or negative associations in service firms. Ittner and Larcker (1998) found that customer satisfaction was positively related to customer retention, revenues and revenue changes for service firms. They also found that the impact of increasing levels of satisfaction was positively and linearly related to improved financial performance up to a threshold, where it diminished in its impact on retention, revenue and revenue change within a telecommunication firm.

A number of specific marketing efforts have been shown to lead to improved satisfaction, which subsequently enhanced performance. Rucci, Kirn and Quinn (1998) found that enhanced customer service levels (achieved through improved employee attitudes) lead to increases in revenue growth at a major department store chain. Additionally, Behn and Riley (1999) found that decreases in customer service at airlines (the quality of baggage handling and overselling of tickets) decreased customer satisfaction, which lead to decreased profitability. Enhanced performance is attributable to both direct effects, through customer loyalty and subsequent purchase behaviors like cross-selling and upgrading of existing customers (Ittner and Larcker, 1998), and indirect effects, due to positive word-of-mouth which generates new customers (Zeithaml, Rust and Lemon, 2001).

Rust, Lemon and Zeithaml (2000) provide a means to estimate the effect of investments in different programs, using their customer equity framework to determine the impact on ROI. For example, they calculated that an investment by Alamo Rental Cars of $60,000 in loyalty programs would yield nearly 31% ROI, a good investment. Another example is that an investment of $60 million in improving service quality at Delta Airlines would yield an ROI of 53%. This framework can also alert managers to possible poor investments. For example, an investment of $1.5 million in improved customer service at Best Buy would result in a −5% ROI. Using their framework can provide insights as to the comparative return from various proposed investments in programs that impact customer loyalty across a variety of industries.

IMPLICATIONS AND RESEARCH AVENUES

To be successful, customer satisfaction and loyalty programs must be integrated throughout the organization. Just as manufacturing developed organizational structures to accommodate zero deficiencies, so should the firm design entire business systems around customer loyalty, such as paying employees based on customer retention units (Reichheld 1993). Emphasizing the importance of coordinating the functions of different departments, Reichheld (1994) identified four basic tools for managing loyalty:

1. Develop measurement systems based on retention.
2. Develop customer targeting based on lifetime value.
3. Conduct ongoing defection analyses.
4. Revise the value proposition accordingly.

Collectively, these are a means of coordinating a unique value proposition to drive superior value and earn loyalty.

Retention-Based Measurement

In the e-commerce environment, it is important to gain consensus on the major drivers of satisfaction and loyalty and then to develop consistent methods for measuring these factors. In addition to tracking purchase information, firms should track number of visitors, frequency of access by specific visitors, abandonment rates, time on site and rate of return to the site (Rosen 2001). Although the means of tracking different patterns of behavior are widely available, it is surprising that companies do not make better use of data capture technologies. Reichheld and Schefter (2000), for example, found that fewer than 20% of firms on the Internet tracked retention rigorously, and many do not even make the attempt to learn from patterns of defection.

It is also important to measure the responsiveness of consumers to different retention and loyalty efforts. Reichheld (1994) encourages the use of metrics to measure customer lifetime value and calculate the impact of increased retention on profits. Zeithaml, Rust and Lemon (2001) found that investments to improve service quality produced greater financial returns when targeted toward the top customer profitability tier (the 20% most profitable) of a major U.S. bank than the bottom tier (bottom 20%). Companies involved in e-commerce should follow suit and develop methods of calculating the impact of various retention-enhancing expenditures on their own customer segments.

Research on building loyalty and assessing performance metrics would enable firms to more effectively allocate their resources. It is possible that certain personality or psychographic characteristics can be associated with lesser or greater degrees of loyalty. If so, firms can direct their efforts to maintaining customers who are loyal by nature and redirect funds now aimed at others.

Targeting Based on Lifetime Value

Reichheld and Schefter (2000) emphasize the importance of focusing on the right customers, those to whom the company can develop a compelling offering that results in high levels of customer loyalty. The logic is straightforward–focus on a key customer segment and develop an appropriate web site with a simple easy-to-use design that loads fast. Schultz and Bailey (2000) suggest that the strength of the relationship depends on two major factors. First, the customer should represent value to the firm. Second, the offering should be compatible with the customer's needs. This involves an understanding of the major drivers, which sometimes differ for different customer groups. For example, Zeithaml, Rust and Lemon (2001) found that *speed* was the major driver for the top customer profitability tier for a major U.S. bank, whereas *attitude* was the major driver for the bottom tier. It is important, therefore, to delineate different groups of consumers and to understand the drivers of value for each of those different groups.

Defection Analyses

Defection analyses should assess which customers have defected and determine the reasons why, but they should also monitor existing customers for drops in spending as a way of tracking changing needs before customers defect. Coyles and Gokey (2002) indicate that tracking downward migration is particularly important for retailing firms because customers typically deal with more than one company. In the banking industry, for example, they found that the 5% of checking account defectors caused a 3% decrease in total balances, whereas the 35% who migrated by reducing their balances cost the bank 24% of its total balances. Thus, there is great opportunity to increase performance by reversing downward trends in spending before customers completely defect.

In traditional markets, it is very easy for service failures to go undetected. Tracking consumer behavior of Internet exchanges provides the opportunity for early detection of problems. Because electronic controls make early intervention possible, research on detection of failures is needed. On the behavioral side, research must determine the most effective ways to reduce defection and attain customer satisfaction.

Revising the Value Proposition

Research by Szymanski and Hise (2000) suggests that customer satisfaction can be enhance via the Internet by focusing on facets such as online convenience, merchandising, site design, and financial security. Also important to consumers is an attractive site, with ease of navigation and visual impact (Licata 2000). Companies should regularly re-evaluate the key drivers of loyalty and revise the fundamental value proposition accordingly (Reichheld 1994).

A number of on-line loyalty incentives can augment the value proposition. Some include discounts, give-aways, contests, sweepstakes and free shipping (Licata 2000). For example, Petopia.com provides the chance for regular shoppers to save 10% on purchases. Gift reminders can also increase purchases by existing customers. Gap.com, for example, allows customers to store information about 10 different people in order to provide reminders of specified gift-giving occasions. Individual firms should identify the most important programs for satisfying their core customers by understanding what it is that they desire in terms of core features, in addition to ways to augment their value propositions.

Getting customers comfortable with Internet transactions is the first hurdle. Customers are asked to trust Internet firms more than their brick and mortar counterparts. Research that identifies the fears of Internet users is needed. As Dell On-Line and others have experienced, the risks of disclosure of credit card information are a major concern and resultant deterrent for Internet users. Credit card companies have used add-on hardware and revolving credit card account numbers to address the fears of their consumers. Such solutions are useful in relationship building by reducing risk perceptions and enhancing the value proposition.

CONCLUSIONS

As many on-line businesses can painfully attest, it is imperative that Internet endeavors be carefully executed with the goal of building customer relationships. The evidence is overwhelming that simply coming into the market with low prices is not a successful strategy. There will always be competitors, albeit with short tenures, that can come in and offer even lower prices. Marketing on the Internet is relatively new, and what we learned from early research already has to be rewritten, incorporating what we learned from the failures of the New Economy as well as new research. Therefore, in this paper, we have proposed a framework for building loyalty via the Internet.

REFERENCES

Anderson, F. W., C. Fornell and D. R. Lehmann (1994), "Customer Satisfaction, Market Share, and Profitability: Findings From Sweden," *Journal of Marketing Research* (July), 53-66.

Baker, Julie, Dhruv Grewal and Michael Levy (1992), "An Experimental Approach to Making Retail Store Environmental Decisions," *Journal of Retailing*, 68 (Winter) 445-460.

Baker, Julie, Dhruv Grewal and A. Parasuraman (1994), "The Influence of Store Environment on Quality Inferences and Store Image," *Journal of the Academy of Marketing Science*, 22:4, 328-339.

Baker, Julie, A. Parasuraman, Dhruv Grewal and Glenn Voss (2002), "The Influence of Multiple Store Environment Cues on Perceived Merchandise Value and Patronage Intentions," *Journal of Marketing*, 66 (April), 120-141.

Baker, W., Marn, M. and Zawada, C. (2001), "Price smarter on the net," *Harvard Business Review*, Vol. 79, February, pp. 122-127.

Behn, Bruce K. and Richard A. Riley Jr. (1999), "Using Nonfinancial Information to Predict Financial Performance: The Case of the U. S. Airline Industry," *Journal of Accounting, Auditing and Finance*, Vol.14 Issue 1 (Winter), 29-56.

Berry, Leonard, Kathleen Seiders and Dhruv Grewal (2002), "Understanding Service Convenience," *Journal of Marketing*, 66 (July), 1-17.

Bhatnagar, Amit, Sanjog Misra and H. Raghav Rao (2000), "On Risk, Convenience, and Internet Shopping Behavior," *Communications of the ACM*, 43 (November), 98-105.

Chain Store Age (2001), "Staples Touts Kiosk, POS Link," *Chain Store Age*, July, 66.

Cimino, Ken (2000), "The Need for Speed," *Siliconvalley.internet.com*, June 15.

Coyles, Stephanie and Timothy C. Gokey (2002), "Customer Retention is Not Enough," *The McKinsey Quarterly*, Vol. 2, available at *www.mckinseyquarterly.com*.

CyberAtlas (1999), "Report on Internet Security", *http://www.cyberatlas.internet.com/resources*.

Dodds, William B., Kent B. Monroe and Dhruv Grewal (1991), "Effects of Price, Brand, and Store Information on Buyers' Product Evaluations," *Journal of Marketing Research*, 28 (August), 307-19.

Ferrell, O. C., Michael D. Hartline, George H. Lucas, Jr., and David Luck (1998). *Marketing Strategy*. Orlando: Harcourt.

Goldman Sachs Investment Research (2000), *Internet Retailing*, Goldman Sachs.

Goodwin, Cathy (1991), "Privacy: Recognition of a Consumer Right," *Journal of Public Policy and Marketing*, 12 (Spring), 106-119.

Grewal, Dhruv, Jerry Gotlieb and Howard Marmorstein (1994), "The Moderating Effects of Message Framing and Source Credibility on the Price-Perceived Risk Relationship," *Journal of Consumer Research*, 21 (June), 145-153.

Grewal, Dhruv, Gopalkrishnan R. Iyer and Michael Levy (2003), "Internet Retailing: Enablers, Limiters and Market Consequences," *Journal of Business Research*, forthcoming.

Grewal, Dhruv, Michael Levy and Greg W. Marshall (2003), "Personal Selling in Retail Settings: How Does the Internet and Related Technologies Enable and Limit Successful Selling? *Journal of Marketing Management,* forthcoming.

Grewal, Dhruv, Kent B. Monroe and R. Krishnan (1998), "The Effects of Price Comparison Advertising on Buyers' Perceptions of Acquisition Value and Transaction Value," *Journal of Marketing,* 62 (April), 46-59.

Grewal, Dhruv, Jeanne Munger, Gopalkrishnan R. Iyer and Michael Levy (2003), "The Influence of Internet-Retailing Factors on Price Expectations," *Psychology & Marketing,* 20 (6), 477-492.

Heskett, James L., W. Earl Sasser, Jr. and Leonard A. Schlesinger (1997), *The Service Profit Chain: How Leading Companies Link Profit and Growth to Loyalty, Satisfaction, and Value.* New York: The Free Press.

Ittner, Christopher D. and David F. Larcker (1998), "Are Nonfinancial Measures Leading Indicators of Financial Performance? An Analysis of Customer Satisfaction," *Journal of Accounting Research,* Vol. 35 (Supplement), 1-35.

Iyer, Gopalkrishnan R., Anthony D. Miyazaki, Dhruv Grewal and Maria Giordano (2002), "Linking Web-Based Segmentation to Pricing Tactics," *Journal of Product & Brand Management,* 11 (5), 288-300.

Jones, Thomas O. and E. Earl Sasser Jr. (1995), "Why Satisfied Customers Defect," *Harvard Business Review,* (November/December), 88-99.

Levy, Michael and Barton A. Weitz (2001), *Retailing Management,* 4th Edition.

Licata, Maureen (2000), "Internet Retailers Shift Focus from Attracting to Retaining On-Line Customers," *Stores,* June, 66-72.

Lisanti, Tony, "Who's Who in Retail–a Preview," *DSN Retailing Today,* 40, no. 1, January 1, 2001, p. 14.

Lohse, Gerald L. and Peter Spiller (1999), "Internet Retail Store Design: How the User Interface Influences Traffic and Sales," *Journal of Computer-Mediated Communication,* [Online] 5 (2), *http://www.ascusc.org/jcmc/vol5/issue2/*

Merrick, Amy. "Keep it Fresh," *The Asian Wall Street Journal,* 10 December 2001, T-10.

Montoya-Weiss, Mitzi, Glenn B. Voss and Dhruv Grewal (2002), "Bricks and Clicks: What Drives Consumers' Use of the Online Channel and Overall Satisfaction in a Multichannel Context?" unpublished working paper, NC: N.C. State University.

Nielsen, Jakob (1997), "Loyalty on the Web," *Alertbox,* August, 1-3.

Novak, Thomas P., Donna L. Hoffman, and Marcos Peralta (1999), "Building Consumer Trust in Online Environments: The Case for Information Privacy," *Communications of the ACM,* 42 (4), 80-85.

Novak, Thomas P., Donna L. Hoffman, and Yiu-Fai Yung (2000), "Measuring the Customer's Experience in Online Environments: A Structural Modeling Approach," *Marketing Science,* 19(1), 22-42.

Parasuraman, A. and Dhruv Grewal (2000), "The Impact of Technology on the Quality-Value-Loyalty Chain: A Research Agenda," *Journal of the Academy of Marketing Science,* 28 No. 1, 168-174.

Peterson, Robert A., Sridhar Balasubramanian, Bart J. Bronnenberg (1997), "Exploring the Implications of the Internet for Consumer Marketing," *Journal of the Academy of Marketing Sciences,* 25 (4), 329-346.

Porter, Michael E. (2001), "Strategy and the Internet," *Harvard Business Review*, March, 63-78.

Reichheld, Frederick F. (1993), "Loyalty-Based Management,"*Harvard Business Review*, March/April, 64-73.

Reichheld, Frederick F. (1994), "Loyalty and the Renaissance of Marketing," *Marketing Management*, 2 (4), 10-21.

Reichheld, Frederick F. and Phil Schefter (2000), E-Loyalty, *Harvard Business Review*, July-August, 105-113.

Rucci, Anthony J., Richard T. Quinn, Steven P. Kirn (1998), "The Employee-Customer-Profit Chain at Sears," *Harvard Business Review*, (January/February), 83-97.

Rosen, Sheri (2001), "Sticky Website is Key to Success," *Communication World*, April-May.

Rust, Roland T. and Katherine N. Lemon (2001), "E-Service and the Consumer," *International Journal of Electronic Commerce*, Spring, 85-101.

Rust, Roland T., Valarie Zeithaml, and Katherine N. Lemon (2000), *Driving Customer Equity*, New York: Free Press.

Scheraga, Dan (2000), "Penney's Net Advantage," *Chain Store Age*, September, 114-118.

Schultz, Don E. and Scott Bailey (2000), "Customer/Brand Loyalty in an Interactive Marketplace," *Journal of Advertising Research*, May-June, 41-52.

Shapiro, Carl and Hal R. Varian (1999), *Information Rules*, Cambridge, MA: Harvard Business School Press.

Sirohi, Niren, Edward W. McLaughlin, and Dick R. Wittink (1998), "A Model of Consumer Perceptions and Store Loyalty Intentions for a Supermarket Retailers," *Journal of Retailing*, 74 (2), 223-245.

Slywotsky, Adrian J. (2000), "The Age of the Choiceboard," *Harvard Business Review*, 78/1 (January/February), pp. 40-41.

Spiller, Peter and Gerald L. Lohse (1998), "A Classification of Internet Retail Stores," *Journal of Electronic Commerce*, 2(2), 29-56.

Szymanski, David M. and Richard T. Hise (2000), "E-Satisfaction: An Initial Examination," *Journal of Retailing*, 76 (3), 309-322.

Tedeschi, Bob (2000), "Easier-to-Use Sites Would Help E-Tailers Close More Sales," *The New York Times*, June 12, C14.

Voss, Glenn, A. Parasuraman and Dhruv Grewal (1998), "The Role of Price and Quality Perceptions in Prepurchase and Postpurchase Evaluation of Services," *Journal of Marketing*, 62 (October), 46-61.

Wingfield, Nick, "Cash Supply Shrinks While Webvan Losses Continue," *The Wall Street Journal*, January 25, 2001, p. B1, B4.

Wang, Huaiqing, Mathew K. O. Lee and Chen Wang (1998), "Consumer Privacy Concerns About Internet Marketing," *Communications of the ACM*, 41 (March), 63-70.

Winer, Russell S. (2001), "A Framework for Customer Relationship Management," *California Management Review*, Vol. 43, No. 4 (Summer) 89-105.

Zeithaml, Valarie, Roland T. Rust and Katherine N. Lemon (2001), "The Customer Pyramid: Creating and Serving Profitable Customers," *California Management Review*, Vol. 43, Issue 4, 118-142.

The Survival
of Internet-Based B2B Exchanges:
The Critical Role of Relationships

Kishore Gopalakrishna Pillai

University of Miami

Arun Sharma

University of Miami

SUMMARY. Researchers have suggested that businesses are undergoing a paradigm shift due to the emergence of the Internet. In the business-to-business arena, fundamental process changes are taking place due to the emergence of Internet-based B2B exchanges. Three types of B2B exchanges have emerged–independent or third party industry specific B2B exchanges, buyer or supplier coalition-based B2B exchanges, and corporate B2B exchanges. While the costs savings associated with Internet-based B2B exchanges are well understood, this paper highlights the critical role that relationships will play in the success or failure of B2B exchanges. Using transactional cost framework, we analyze the various types of Internet-based B2B exchanges and conclude that corpo-

---

Kishore Gopalakrishna Pillai is a PhD student and Arun Sharma is Professor of Marketing, both at the University of Miami.

Address correspondence to: Arun Sharma, Department of Marketing, University of Miami, P.O. Box 248147, Coral Gables, FL 33124 (E-mail: asharma@miami.edu).

[Haworth co-indexing entry note]: "The Survival of Internet-Based B2B Exchanges: The Critical Role of Relationships." Pillai, Kishore Gopalakrishna, and Arun Sharma. Co-published simultaneously in *Journal of Relationship Marketing* (Best Business Books, an imprint of The Haworth Press, Inc.) Vol. 2, No. 3/4, 2003, pp. 51-65; and: *Customer Relationship Management in Electronic Markets* (ed: Gopalkrishnan R. Iyer, and David Bejou) Best Business Books, an imprint of The Haworth Press, Inc., 2003, pp. 51-65. Single or multiple copies of this article are available for a fee from The Haworth Document Delivery Service [1-800-HAWORTH, 9:00 a.m. - 5:00 p.m. (EST). E-mail address: docdelivery@haworthpress.com].

Digital Object Identifier: 10.1300/J366v02n03_04

rate exchanges have a comparative advantage over open market exchanges, as well as over buyer or supplier coalition-based exchanges. It is our expectation that this paper will serve as a catalyst for future research in this area. *[Article copies available for a fee from The Haworth Document Delivery Service: 1-800-HAWORTH. E-mail address: <docdelivery@ haworthpress.com> Website: <http://www.HaworthPress.com> © 2003 by The Haworth Press, Inc. All rights reserved.]*

KEYWORDS. B2B exchanges, relationship success, governance costs, transaction costs, coalition-based exchanges

INTRODUCTION

The growth in the adoption of the Internet in B2B marketing has been revolutionary in the last decade. B2B transactions are expected to be in the range of $800 billion dollars by the year 2003–five times as much as business-to-consumer transactions. The primary impetus for the move toward the Internet is the value that can be generated. Since the Internet can be used to reduce the "exchange friction" that exists both within and between organizations, business marketers can better deliver value to their customers.

The growth of the Internet has led to an interesting development in the B2B domain. There has been growth of Internet-based B2B exchanges (hereafter referred to as B2B exchanges), which are equivalent to electronic marketplaces. The analog of B2B exchanges are specialized markets such as antique shows where both buyers and sellers function. The primary advantage is a reduction of prices due to open market conditions, and a reduction in transaction costs due to the utilization of the Internet to conduct transactions. The first entries to the world of B2B exchanges were independent or third party exchanges that concentrated in either one industry (e.g., Plasticsnet.com) or in multiple industries (e.g., Verticalnet.com). Although regarded as disruptive change agents in the initial stages, most independent or third party exchanges have not succeeded. The second stage of growth of B2B exchanges emerged from either buyers (e.g., automobile manufacturers) or suppliers (e.g., memory chip manufacturers) creating B2B exchanges. The development of these B2B exchanges has been slow and the success is not assured. The third stage of development is in the area of corporate-based B2B exchanges, in which a firm uses the Internet-based B2B exchange to conduct supplier transactions. These exchanges have been successful as firms such as Dell, IBM and Intel are conducting over $1 billion worth of transactions from this platform. This paper attempts to understand the underlying reasons for the success and failure of B2B exchanges. We apply both the transactional cost theory and relationship theories to better understand the mechanisms of B2B exchanges. The first section discusses the growth of B2B exchanges. The second section applies transactional cost theory with specific application of relationship theories. Our conclusions are presented in the subsequent section followed by implications for research and practice.

B2B BUYING EXCHANGES

The first stage of growth in any substantial manner was generated by third party or neutral B2B exchanges. These exchanges billed themselves as electronic market places where buyers and sellers could meet. Sellers would have a better understanding of market movements and buyers could get a lower price due to open bidding. These firms envisioned buying firms provisioning from a wide variety of sources that were transactional/relational or domestic/global. Some of the B2B exchanges were industry-specific (Ultraprise.com-mortgages; Plasticsnet. com–plastics), and some were business marketplaces for a variety of industries (Verticalnet.com). The industry-specific exchanges also began providing such information as job placement advice/updates and technical manuals to the industry. Most of the first wave of firms did not survive. Of the firms that we mentioned, Ultraprise.com was bought for its IT assets, and Plasticsnet.com was bought by Verticalnet.com, and Verticalnet.com is repositioning itself as a supply chain solution provider.

The next stage of growth came from buying networks. Buying consortia established these exchanges. The advantage of these exchanges was the power they provided buyers over sellers, as buyers were the focal point in this system. These exchanges were created to take advantage of the buying power of firms to obtain lower costs. In addition, savings were expected from transactional cost reductions due to the processing over the Internet. Examples of these exchanges are Covisint. com, created for the auto industry by the auto majors, Converge.com for high tech buyers and sellers, Exostar.com for aerospace and defense industries, and Novopoint.com for the food and beverage industry (Grimes,

2001). Morgan Stanley estimates that B2B as applied within Covisint and forecast to be the Internet's largest commercial operation, will save Ford, GM and Daimler Chrysler US $2,700 per vehicle. Unfortunately, these firms have had a very difficult time getting started and the savings are yet to be seen.

The third major growth in B2B exchanges emerged from corporations. Firms that had implemented supply chain platforms such as SAP found it easy to extend the platform to the web. Early adopters of this technology were firms such as Cisco, IBM, and Dell. In addition, firms also started developing selling exchanges that could be easily tied into their buying exchanges. For examples, Dell and GE have both buying and selling corporate exchanges (e.g., GE Polymerland). The primary advantage is to reduce costs through lower cost of transaction processing, as well as better cost control through better demand-supply management. These corporate exchanges have been extremely successful.

In the next section, we discuss some possible reasons for the apparent success of corporate exchanges and the difficulty that third party and buyer exchanges are undergoing.

THE CRITICAL ROLE
OF RELATIONSHIPS IN B2B TRANSACTIONS

We believe that one of the fallacies of B2B exchanges was the assumption that there are no differences between transactional and relational customers. Sheth and Sharma (1997) highlighted some of the reasons for enhanced relationship between buyers and suppliers. The primary reasons for the increasing dependence of buyers on suppliers are:

- Maintaining supplier relationships is expensive and most firms have fewer suppliers than ten years ago.
- With enhanced competition, both locally and globally, enhanced supplier relationships lead to better market positioning.
- With lean inventories associated with just-in-time or demand-driven manufacturing, supplier commitment is critical.

Sheth and Sharma (1997) provide data from the Japanese automobile industry, Eastman Kodak, Ford Motor Company, Levi Strauss, DuPont, McKesson, and Bose Corporation to demonstrate savings associated with supplier relationships.

Sheth and Sharma (1997) also suggest that buyer-supplier relationships are critical because they incorporate:

- Trust and Commitment to Long-Term Goals.
- Mutual Benefit.
- Top Management Support.
- Compatible Organizational Culture.
- Sharing of Information.
- Strong and Open Communications.

The incorporation of the above mentioned characteristics into buyer-supplier relationships have an effect of decreasing the need of monitoring the performance of the exchange partner. This leads to reduced monitoring costs and better supply chain management. Unfortunately, transactional customers do not demonstrate the above-mentioned relational properties leading to increased monitoring requirements and higher monitoring costs. We seek to demonstrate in subsequent sections, why this lack of commitment may lead to the lack of success of some types of B2B exchanges.

UNDERSTANDING B2B EXCHANGES–
A TRANSACTIONAL COST FRAMEWORK

We use transactional cost theory to analyze B2B exchanges. The theory was developed in the context of vertical exchanges or markets. We apply the theory to understanding the differences in cost structures between traditional purchasing and B2B exchanges. Similar applications of transactional cost analysis have been observed in several studies in sales and channel management (e.g., Anderson 1985; Sharma and Dominguez 1992).

Transactional cost analysis examines "the comparative costs of planning, adapting, and monitoring task completion under alternative governance structures" (Williamson 1983, p. 104). The underlying principle is that a firm will perform a task internally if it has a total cost advantage over the marketplace. Transactional cost analysis explicitly recognizes governance costs in addition to production/exchange costs. Production/exchange costs are those associated with the production/exchange of the product or service. Governance or "control" costs are those associated with planning, executing, and monitoring performance. The make-or-buy decision, which forms the focal decision around which the theory is structured, hinges on the balance between internal and external costs in these two categories, i.e.:

ΔC = Internal production costs – External exchange costs
ΔG = Internal governance costs – External governance costs

When the sum of these categories is positive, i.e., when:

$$\Delta C + \Delta G > 0,$$

it will be more costly to produce internally; the function will be assigned to the market place. However, when the sum is negative, i.e., when:

$$\Delta C + \Delta G < 0,$$

firms will internalize the function (Sharma and Dominguez 1992).

Three factors of interest in this context are critical in determining the value of $\Delta C + \Delta G$, and hence the extent of reliance on the marketplace. They are asset specificity, volume, and externalities of "quality debasement" or product/service quality control (Williamson 1983). Suppliers have certain specialized tangible and intangible assets that are critical to a manufacturer (Anderson and Coughlan 1987; Williamson 1983). These specialized assets are advantageous site or location, specialized physical facilities (e.g., production facilities), and human assets (e.g., personnel with specialized skills). When assets are very non-specific, producers can easily replace suppliers. The more specific assets required, the lower the value of $\Delta C + \Delta G$, giving the marketer an incentive to perform the function internally (Williamson 1981). The reasons for this are: (a) the cost of specific assets cannot be shared with other products, thereby reducing the cost advantage of the marketplace; and (b) specific assets increase the need for control, increasing the cost of external governance. Studies have found that asset specificity leads to increased internalization of partner functions (Anderson 1985; Anderson and Coughlan 1987; John and Weitz 1988; Klein, Frazier and Roth 1990).

The second factor is supply volume. Increased volume stimulates internalization of functions (Anderson 1985; Klein, Frazier and Roth 1990). Transactional cost analysis accounts for this phenomenon through two mechanisms: (a) with increasing volume, individual firms can attain sufficient economies of scale that the difference between internal and external costs diminishes, thereby reducing ΔC (Klein, Frazier and Roth 1990; Williamson 1981); and (b) economies of scale reduce the cost of internal governance (Anderson 1985).

Quality debasement externalities arise with products that are expensive and complex, whose quality cannot be easily monitored. It becomes more difficult to monitor suppliers' compliance with producers' standards. As a result, external governance costs will rise for those products (Anderson 1985; Bowen and Jones 1986; John and Weitz 1988), thereby reducing the value of ΔG, and thus $\Delta C + \Delta G$. Hence, firms are likely to create relationships with suppliers with increasing demand for goods that involve high asset specificity and quality debasement externalities.

B2B Exchanges

We apply the basic principles of transactional cost theory to B2B exchanges, examining the case of traditional purchasing and comparing it to different forms of B2B exchanges. Transaction cost theory lends itself to an understanding of the comparative advantages of each of the different types of B2B exchanges.

We examine the costs across a variety of parameters relevant to a buyer-supplier relationship. Two aspects of transactional costs are discussed separately in the context of our discussion of the three B2B exchanges.

Our analysis is based on the perspective of the buyer (cf, Cannon and Perreault Jr. 1999). The rationale for the buyer perspective lies in the fact that it is usually the customer who ultimately makes the decision of whether to list requirements on a B2B exchange. Our analytical model accounts for the sellers' viewpoint also. The seller's viewpoint is captured in the dimensions that we borrowed from the enhanced TCA model, which focus on the reciprocity between buyer and seller. Thus, our analysis attempts to incorporate both economizing aspect through traditional transaction cost perspective, and relational aspects. We provide a summary of our discussion in Table 1.

Exchange Costs

Within exchange costs, we look at buying price, which accounts for the price at which the product or service is purchased, and transaction

TABLE 1. Comparison of the B2B Exchanges

	Traditional Buying	Third-Party	Buying Groups	Corporate Exchanges
Acquisition Cost				
Buying price	Medium	Low	Low- medium	Medium
Transaction costs	Medium	Low	Low	Low
Governance Cost				
Transaction monitoring cost	Low	High	Medium	Low
Quality debasement	Low	High	Low-medium	Low
Length of relationship	High	Low	Medium	High
Mutual dependence	High	Low	Medium	High
Cost of ensuring privacy	Low	High	High	Low

costs that include costs incurred in inviting the supplier, placing orders, and processing payments.

Buying Price: We suggest that traditional buying has medium costs. Firms predominantly buy from existing suppliers, and evidence suggests that their prices may not be the lowest. In third-party markets, we expect the prices to be the lowest. Open markets allow all suppliers to bid, which should lead to lower prices. The reason is that firms that do not have a relationship with large users may attempt to develop a relationship through cheaper prices. In addition, quality will be unknown at this stage leading to a reduction in prices. Monitoring quality is an issue that we will discuss in the next section.

Buying groups, due to the merging of demand, will have lower prices than traditional buying. However, since some quality control will be implemented for inclusion as suppliers, the prices may not be as low as open markets. Finally, we expect corporate exchanges to have the same prices as traditional buying, as the supplier bases are the same.

Transaction Costs: Transaction costs are medium under traditional buying, since much data entry and payment processing work is done manually (Sharma 2002). We expect the utilization of an Internet-based platform to reduce transactional costs and errors in the three types of exchanges.

Governance Costs

We examine the factors that affect governance costs in the B2B exchange context. First, we examine transaction monitoring costs–preventing opportunism and bounded rationality; and quality debasement as suggested by Williamson (1981). We also borrow some antecedents proposed by Palmatier (2002) in his attempt to integrate relevant aspects of reciprocal altruism into the TCA framework. These antecedents are length of relationship and mutual dependence. Finally, we examine a unique factor that comes in play in the Internet arena–the issue of privacy of information.

Transaction Monitoring Costs: Transaction monitoring includes the costs incurred in limiting partner opportunism in transactions and in overcoming the limitations of bounded rationality. These costs are associated with ensuring that exchange partners do not seek to take advantage of other partners. Traditional buying has incorporated relationships with suppliers. In this case, due to the reasons outlined in previous sections, transaction monitoring costs are low. In third-party markets, these costs are expected to be high, specifically in cases where the buyer has no previous experience with the supplier. In buying groups, transaction monitoring costs are expected to be medium. The reason is that even if the buyer has no previous experience with the supplier, some prescreening has been done by the exchange. In corporate exchanges, due to existing relationships, we do not expect transaction monitoring costs to rise. In fact, there may be a cost reduction due to the use of technology. Therefore, in corporate B2B exchanges, governance monitoring costs are expected to be low.

Quality Debasement: Quality debasement is likely to be low in traditional buying processes. The reason is that firms have developed existing relationships, incorporate relational properties and therefore quality debasement is low. In third-party B2B exchanges, we expect quality debasement to be high because of the short term, transactional or non-screened nature of the interactions. In buying group exchanges quality debasement should be medium (lower than third party exchanges), due to the pre-screening of suppliers. In corporate exchanges, we expect quality debasement to be low, equivalent to traditional buying relationships.

Length of Relationship: Length of relationship is expected to affect governance costs. Based on our discussions in previous sections, we expect length of relationship to be negatively correlated with governance costs. Length of relationship is expected to be high in traditional buying, leading to lower governance costs. The nature of third-party exchanges (open markets) will shorten the length of relationships, increasing governance costs. We expect length of relationship to be medium in buying group exchanges, as there will be a mix of existing and new suppliers. Therefore, governance costs will be medium. Finally, we expect length of relationship to be high in corporate exchanges leading to low governance costs.

Mutual Dependence: Mutual dependence leads to mutual growth that leads to more altruistic behavior (Palmatier 2002), and is expected to reduce governance costs. Mutual dependence is lowest in third-party B2B exchanges, medium in buying group exchanges, and high in traditional buying and corporate exchanges. Therefore, governance costs are expected to be highest in third-party B2B exchanges, medium in buying group exchanges, and lowest in traditional buying and corporate exchanges.

Cost of Ensuring Privacy: Trust and privacy issues have been a concern with Internet business (Hoffman, Novak and Peralta, 1999; Korgaonkar and Wolin, 1999). In B2B exchanges, privacy of data becomes more critical. Open exchange of data from both suppliers and buyers allows competitors to determine firm level strategy. In addition, data allow buyers to be aware of supplier pricing strategies. Therefore, privacy of data is emerging as a major issue in B2B exchanges. The cost of ensuring privacy in third-party B2B exchanges is expected to be high. Buying groups are also expected to have data leakage, leading to high costs of ensuring privacy. Traditional buying and corporate exchanges are expected to have lower costs of ensuring privacy.

COMPARING B2B EXCHANGES

In this section, the three B2B exchanges are compared in the context of transactional costs, i.e., $\Delta C + \Delta G$. The three models are compared on the dimensions discussed in the previous section. We provide the summarized figure in Figure 1. The three models are compared to traditional buying processes, and the classic transactional cost equations are reformulated as:

ΔC = Traditional-buying acquisition costs $-$ B2B exchange acquisition costs

ΔG = Traditional-buying governance costs $-$ B2B exchange governance costs

When the sum of these categories is positive, i.e., when:

$$\Delta C + \Delta G > 0$$

firms will use B2B exchanges. However, when the sum is negative, i.e., when:

$$\Delta C + \Delta G < 0$$

firms will continue to use traditional buying processes.

Third-Party or Open B2B Exchange

Third-party exchanges provide lower exchange costs due to open bidding. Therefore, ΔC is positive and large. In contrast, governance costs associated with unknown suppliers are expected to be high. In addition, privacy of data will remain a major issue. Therefore, ΔG is expected to be negative and very large. Therefore, $\Delta C + \Delta G$ is expected to be negative, leading to firms not choosing third party exchanges. This finding is supported with data shown in the previous discussion of the failure of a large number of third-party B2B exchanges. Recent reports examining the causes of the failure of third party Internet-based B2B

FIGURE 1. Cost Structures

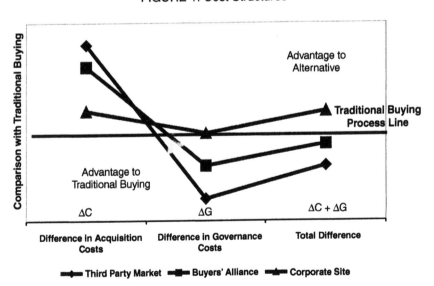

exchange arena offers the following possible causes (Lentz 2000; Sawhney 2002):

- The philosophy of minimal purchasing price. Since price is only one part of the total supply chain process, value is derived from optimizing the costs in the entire system.
- Third-party B2B exchanges used the perspective of the buyer with no incentives for the seller.
- Exchanges were predominantly e-catalogues, and there was a lack of supply chain processes such as inventory level monitoring, payments, and reconciliations.
- Focus should have been on improving the efficiency and effectiveness of the interaction rather than on finding new suppliers or buyers.

Buying Group B2B Exchanges

Buying group exchanges provide lower exchange costs due to buying volumes. Therefore, ΔC is positive. In contrast, governance costs associated with a mixture of known and unknown suppliers are expected to be higher than traditional purchasing. In addition, privacy of data from competitors will remain a major issue. Therefore, ΔG is expected to be negative and large, and $\Delta C + \Delta G$ is expected to be negative, leading to firms not choosing buying group exchanges. This finding is supported by data presented in a previous discussion of the slow progress of a large number of buying-group B2B exchanges. For example, when asked the reasons for not joining Covisint, automotive suppliers who opted out mentioned (*www.sme.org*):

- Don't see benefits (37%).
- Lack of company infrastructure (28%).
- Lack of privacy (24%).

Therefore, customers of a buyers network are anxious that their data does not go into the hands of their competitors. Based on the analysis, we expect buyer group B2B exchanges to have problems in succeeding. We see some evidence of this phenomenon as Volkswagen has created a corporate B2B exchange rather than join Covisint.

Corporate B2B Exchanges

Corporate B2B exchanges provide lower exchange costs due to lower transaction costs. Therefore, ΔC is positive. Governance costs associated with relational suppliers are expected to be similar to traditional purchasing. Use of technology may reduce some governance costs. In addition, privacy of data is not an issue. Therefore, ΔG is expected to be zero or slightly positive, so that $\Delta C + \Delta G$ is expected to be positive, leading to firms choosing corporate B2B exchanges. We have evidence of the success of corporate exchanges over other types of exchanges. In the plastics industry, the on-line marketer Ventro did $100 million business in 2001, in contrast to a corporate exchange GE Polymerland that did $1.5 billion. In the electronics industry, VerticalNet did $125.6 million business in 2001 in comparison with Cisco, IBM, and Intel, that did up to $2 billion per month in business.

CONCLUSION

This paper examines B2B exchanges and applies relationship and transactional cost analysis to B2B exchanges. The study highlights the critical role of relationship and governance costs in the growth and success of B2B exchanges. Ignoring relational aspects will lead to failure of other models. In addition, governance costs will be critical in the survival of B2B exchanges. In order to survive, buyer group exchanges need to ensure lower governance costs through better screening of suppliers and maintaining privacy of data. If these factors are not controlled, the success of buyer group exchanges is not assured.

We suggest that unless drastic changes are undertaken, third party and buyer exchanges may not be successful. However, we expect corporate B2B exchanges to grow.

Areas of Future Research

The paper discusses an area of fertile research. The application of transactional cost framework is unique in the context of B2B exchanges. In addition, we would suggest the following areas for future research:

- Will the chart presented in Figure 1 maintain in the face of changes that B2B exchanges will incorporate?

- What are the antecedents and consequences of B2B exchanges on relationship marketing?
- What will be rate of increase in B2B exchanges? What industry and business market characteristics will influence the development?
- What technology will enable the movement from traditional buying to corporate B2B exchanges?
- Will corporate B2B exchanges emerge as a core competency in business markets?
- Under what conditions will buyer group B2B exchanges enjoy increased acceptance in business markets?
- Will the nature of the Internet with universal information access, in conjunction with low switching costs, make business relationships difficult to maintain?
- How can business firms increase the switching costs for their customers?
- How critical will face-to-face communication be in the B2B exchange era?
- Will business marketing paradigms evolve from competition-based toward alliance-based rules?
- How will B2B buyer exchanges address antitrust issues?

REFERENCES

Anderson, Erin (1985), "The Salesperson as Outside Agent or Employee: A Transaction Cost Analysis," *Marketing Science*, 4 (Summer), 234-254.

Anderson, Erin and Ann T. Coughlan (1987), "International Market Entry and Expansion via Independent or Integrated Channels of Distribution." *Journal of Marketing*, 51 (January), 71-82.

Bowen, David E. and Gareth R. Jones, (1986), "Transaction Cost Analysis of Service Organization Customer Change," *Academy of Management Review*, 11 (April), 428-441.

Cannon, Joseph P. and William D. Perreault Jr. (1999), "Buyer-Seller Relationships in Business Markets," *Journal of Marketing Research*, xxxvi (November), 439-460.

Grimes, Paul (2000), "Digging Deep for Airfare Deals," *The Globe and Mail*, (November).

Hoffman, D.L., T.P. Novak and M. Peralta (1999), "Building Consumer Trust Online," *Communication of the ACM*, 42, 80-85.

John, George and Barton Weitz (1988), " Forward Integration into Distribution: Empirical Test of Transactional Cost Analysis," *Journal of Law, Economics and Organization*, 4 (Fall), 121-139.

Klein, Saul, Gary Frazier and Victor J. Roth (1990), "A Transactional Cost Model of Channel Integration in International Markets," *Journal of Marketing Research*, 17 (May), 196-208.

Korgaonkar, P.K. and L.D. Wolin (1999), "A Multivariate Analysis of Web Usage," *Journal of Advertising Research*, (March-April), 53-68.

Lentz, Nate (2000), "Beyond the Exchange," *Business 2.0*, (June).

Palmatier, Robert W. (2002), "Enhancing Transaction Cost Analysis with Insights from Sociobiology: Dynamic Tension Between Reciprocal Altruism and Opportunism," Eds. Ken Evans and Lisa Scheer, Proceedings of Winter AMA Conference.

Sawhney, Mohanbir (2002), "Putting the Horse First; B2B Exchanges Failed Because They Got Their Business Models Backward," *CIO*, Framingham (May 15).

Sharma, Arun (2002), "Trends in Internet-Based Business to Business Marketing," *Industrial Marketing Management*, 31, 77-84.

Sharma, Arun and Luis V. Dominguez (1992), "Channel Evolution: A Framework for Analysis," *Journal of the Academy of Marketing Sciences*, 20, 1, 1-15.

Sheth, Jagdish N., and Arun Sharma (1997), "Supplier Relationships: Emerging Issues and Challenges," *Industrial Marketing Management*, 26, 2, 91-100.

Williamson, Oliver E. (1981), "The Economics of Organizations: The Transaction Cost Approach," *American Journal of Sociology*, 87, 3, 548-577.

Williamson, Oliver E. (1983), "Organizational Innovation: The Transactional Cost Approach," In *Entrepreneurship*. Ed. Joshua Ronen. Lexington, MA: Lexington Books.

Business Buyer Relationship Management Through Seamless Internet Integration

J. David Lichtenthal

Zicklin School of Business

SUMMARY. There is a growing need to look specifically at Internet integration into business relationship management tactics, beyond sustaining current customers. The Internet enables active implementation of a business buyer relationship management (BBRM) orientation through the facilitation of information sharing and buyer connectivity across various buying conditions. Using Internet tools, the goal of merely sustaining present buyers now appears insufficient. BBRM takes into account that these tools must be effectively utilized across a variety of buying situations including how sellers and buyers come together, stay together and inevitably remake their business relationships endure. BBRM makes effective use of Internet technologies despite various buying situations to enable seller-buyer relationship formation, maintenance and long-term continuation. *[Article copies available for a fee from The Haworth Document Delivery Service: 1-800-HAWORTH. E-mail address: <docdelivery@haworthpress.*

J. David Lichtenthal is Editor, *Journal of Business to Business Marketing*, and Professor of Marketing, Zicklin School of Business, Baruch College, City University of New York, 1 Bernard Baruch Way, B 12-240, New York, NY 10010-5518 (E-mail: david_lichtenthal@baruch.cuny.edu).

The author appreciates the partial funding for this research provided by the Institute for the Study of Business Markets at the Pennsylvania State University.

[Haworth co-indexing entry note]: "Business Buyer Relationship Management Through Seamless Internet Integration." Lichtenthal, J. David. Co-published simultaneously in *Journal of Relationship Marketing* (Best Business Books, an imprint of The Haworth Press, Inc.) Vol. 2. No. 3/4, 2003, pp. 67-83; and: *Customer Relationship Management in Electronic Markets* (ed: Gopalkrishnan R. Iyer, and David Bejou) Best Business Books, an imprint of The Haworth Press, Inc., 2003, pp. 67-83. Single or multiple copies of this article are available for a fee from The Haworth Document Delivery Service [1-800-HAWORTH, 9:00 a.m. - 5:00 p.m. (EST). E-mail address: docdelivery@haworthpress.com].

http://www.haworthpress.com/store/product.asp?sku=J366
Digital Object Identifier: 10.1300/J366v02n03_05

com> Website: <http://www.HaworthPress.com> © 2003 by The Haworth Press, Inc. All rights reserved.]

KEYWORDS. Business buyer relationship management, business marketing, customer relationship management, Internet integration, e-commerce, e-business

BACKGROUND

By most measures, barely over a decade old, the Internet is having a profound impact on every aspect of business marketing practice. Enterprises are competing based on relationships, not just the basic products and services buyers have essentially come to expect (Kanter 1994) and most commerce on the Internet remains business-to-business (Reibstein 2000). Much of this commerce represents a shift in the manner of purchasing: businesses are purchasing from the same vendor, but using the Internet rather than the phone or fax to achieve *cost efficiencies*. For example, IBM now requires that all purchases be made electronically.

In the near term, *e-commerce will not be as disruptive* to many traditional buyer-supplier relationships as originally thought, since, companies find that *offline communication is almost always needed to complete online transactions*. Suppliers will continue to send sales staff to court buyers, and buyers will continue to demand personal commitments from their suppliers. However, ongoing relationship management is likely better coordinated on the Internet.

Buyer relationship management is really not so new as the technology that is allowing all firms to do what only the smallest business marketers have always done–know their buyers and associated requirements fully (Morrow 2001, p. 14). For large business marketers, having enough brainpower to keep track of everyone's preferences can now be done to almost any scale. In the past, cost economies were such that account management calculations required that accounts be larger. In the present era, *for many business marketers, there is a greater ability to reach many small as well as large business buyers and serve them well*.

Businesses are learning to compete in the hybrid physical and electronic business market environment, while leveraging the potential of the Internet into all aspects of business buyer acquisition and retention. A growing number of firms are discovering that the potential of the Internet is best exploited by creating seller-buyer partnerships where both parties benefit. The long-term viability of many businesses stems from value-stream robustness which directly influences revenue streams (Mahadevan 2000).

For Internet augmented businesses, a buyer's perceived value arises from effort reduction in product search, reduced transaction and usage costs. Business buyer relationship management *(BBRM) coupled to the Internet inherently yields richness and reach, creating vastly improved buying and selling experiences* effecting the bottom lines of all parties to a relationship. Integrating the Internet into business marketing tactics is integral to long term viability for business marketing in *all* marketing mix areas (Lichtenthal and Eliaz 2002).

Initially, the paper briefly gives an overview of business marketing relationship practices and an expanded view on the fluctuating nature of business market space. Subsequently, the focus of the paper provides an in-depth exploration on Internet utilization for retaining, sustaining and obtaining business buyers. The tactical impact on Internet usage is developed for six classic buying situations business marketers typically face in the markets they serve. Implications for aiding buyer choice process are noted below.

EVOLVING CONTEXT
FOR BUSINESS BUYER RELATIONSHIP MANAGEMENT

Perspective. Business seller-buyer relationships have traditionally strived to be long-term rather than transaction oriented (Hutt and Speh 2001; Kanter 1994). Early on, the predominant company focus was on finding new buyers and closing a sale, a practice that has given way to keeping current buyers and building lasting relationships (see Appendix A for a precis on these perspectives). The primary shift is in the temporal goal, i.e., from making a profit on each sale per se to long term profits through managing the fluctuating net present value of a business buyer's purchases into a longer-term horizon. The Internet typically provides lower contact and transaction costs with greater access for maintaining each business buyer relationship over a much larger customer base. Retention of the existing buyer base remains a key objective (Kropper 2001).

Powered by Software. Revenues for customer relationship management (CRM) software is growing globally and is predicted to be $30.6 billion in 2005 up from $9.4 billion in 2001, according to Cahners In-Stat Group. The compelling reason for the healthy CRM applications market includes the dual corporate requirements of retaining existing buyers while reducing internal costs and streamlining processes. Larger U.S. companies will continue to create the most opportunity for CRM vendors, having spent approximately $1.9 billion in 2001 or about 78 percent of national CRM revenues (*Ibid.*).

Tools tuning into buyers. B2B e-commerce has progressed through several generations (Sawney 2001). The first, electronic data exchange (EDI), involved *one-to-one interactions* by companies transacting with strategic partners and channels. EDI was proprietary, inflexible, rigid and therefore limited to largest sellers and buyers. The second, *one-to-many interactions*, was epitomized by Dell and Cisco selling directly to buyers. Consequently, anyone could transact with their company. The third generation saw the advent of *many-to-many* pubic marketplaces or "hubs" like Transora or Covisint connecting sellers and buyers, while the fourth brought the advent of *private networks,* facilitating buy-side and sell-side interactions with strategic suppliers and channel partners.

The fifth generation, *any-to-any architecture*, is a "superset" that includes *all* previous mechanisms. This is peer-to-peer, where enterprises use Web services to interact dynamically with any other entity facilitated by a central web registry–the Napster model applied to B2B–allowing for real-time construction of modular shared business processes across enterprises. The shift to work flows over transactions will continue as B2B e-commerce is conducted fundamentally through interactions in the context of collaboration (Sawney 2001) among relationship-oriented businesses.

Commercial Consequences. These business phenomena must be seen as evolutionary yet integrative processes spanning several decades (see Table 1). Contemporary analysis suggests three broad eras in approach to e-commerce at the macro-economic level.[1] The genesis for one era starts in the prior era.

In the past, there was a short-term focus with *transactional exchanges* marked by recurring negotiations, consideration and use of many brands as well as minimal information exchange and commitment. The purchase decision was neither complex nor of strategic importance and supply markets were viewed as stable. Subsequently, an intermediate term focus called *collaborative exchange* recognized the value to both sides for repeat business, limited brand consideration and usage, restricted alternatives with less restrictive information exchange and a sense of enduring commitment.

The current era and beyond, *continuous exchange* has a cooperative systems focus, recognizes the almost infinite mutual interdependence

TABLE 1. Buyer Relationship Marketing: Past, Present, Future

Dimensions	<-----1980s-----> Transactional Exchange	<-------1990s--------> Collaborative Exchange	<------2000s--------> Continuous Exchange
Purchase Focus	purchase incidents	repetitive purchasing	alliance
Purchase Importance	lower purchase importance	moderate purchase importance	higher purchase importance
Purchase Time-Frame	negotiated term	intermediate term	seemingly indefinite term
Consideration of Alternatives	many brand alternatives	fewer brand alternatives	focused brand selection
Informational Links	minimal information exchange	ongoing information exchange	exponential information links
Operational Contacts	temporary operational links	temporarily permanent links	coupled operations
Commitment	minimal commitment	considerable commitment	commitment

Sources: Based on an integration of concepts adapted from Narus and Anderson (1991), Webster (1992) and Cannon and Perrault (1999), and Hutt and Speh (2001).

with strong coupling and fosters commitments for multi-level information exchanges and operational linkages. Indeed, to implement a *decision to cease doing business might take months or even years.* The time frames and *costs to uncouple are very high for both sides.* For example, this would likely be the case between chemical companies whose linkages include pipelines as well as computer systems and many interfaces of operations staff. Special assets (economic and social), which are costly to recreate, reduce a propensity toward variety and alternative seeking behavior.

For some business sellers and buyers, the foreseeable future includes focused, if not unique brand usage given the very high level of commitment. With a long-term focus permeating business buyer relations, tactical implications for firms will continue to manifest. Contractual arrangements are common to help ensure both sides of the business seller-buyer dyad fully articulate their needs to each other as well as unto themselves.

View of the Potential Market and Business Buyer Base

The business marketplace is an ever-expanding (and contracting) temporal space, perhaps more so than the geographic and economic boundaries that historically demarcated it (Kotler and Armstrong 2001). The proliferation of e-markets increases the likelihood that those market boundaries are operationally infinite. Some proof can be garnered by viewing business market segment occupancy through the metaphor of a mathematical limit.[2]

Market space (for a segment) can expand "indefinitely," yet can never be fully reached either (membership units are born (and decline or die)), changes in need state and change segments (bases). Operationally, this requires a firm to create and pro-actively seek an optimal buyer base, in geographic, economic and market-cyberspace. This posture must be sustained indefinitely, even though the firm can only *strive but never achieve* market saturation. Marketing effort, in this sense, must be ever-expanding to mirror the seemingly limitless nature of demand in business markets. Otherwise, a business marketer could be lulled into tactical complacency.

Sustaining an intensive strategy for obtaining, sustaining and reclaiming business buyers is necessary to ensure optimal capture of business segment membership which is in constant flux. Even though world population is expanding, replacement populations turn over at varying rates and, *even if both were to go into declining rates*, any given individual firm or group of firms (members of a business market segment) can "move" in and out of the particular market space by virtue of their ever-changing need states and bases for describing their segment occupancy. Hence, segment "full occupancy" is never reached, yet the business marketer *must* continuously try to attain it, from all buyers, regardless of their buying situation.

SUSTAINING, RECLAIMING AND OBTAINING BUSINESS BUYERS

Business buying behavior and the forces affecting it have been examined from many perspectives including how sellers and buyers come together, stay together and break up (Lichtenthal and Shani 2000). Business buyer relationship management overtly recognizes that CRM is only an important subset of a long-term strategy taking into account the full range of buying situations likely to be encountered by most business marketers.

A broader set of buying conditions beyond retention of existing active buyers must be managed. Organizational buying theory has long recognized that business buying situation complexity varies based on need for information and risk reduction (Robinson, Faris and Wind

1967; Doyle, Woodside and Michel 1979; Ferguson 1979; Bellizzi and McVey 1983).

Recently, these buying situations have been rarefied and expanded into six categories from *most to least* complex (i.e., strategic new-task, judgmental new task, complex modified rebuy, simple modified rebuy, routine low priority and casual purchase) business marketers face in the markets they strive to serve (Hutt and Speh 2001). Their complexity differs as does the associated business marketing task. CRM tacitly assumes a condition of routinized response behavior. For firms making optimal use of Internet technology, analysis and application must include obtaining business buyers new to a product class or brand as well as those buyers that periodically need to revise their buying strategy.

Indeed, from the business marketer's viewpoint, an ideal stasis occurs when new buyers become repeat buyers and rarely move on. An effective and efficient BBRM process should aid in the retention, reclamation and acquisition of the business buyer base to be served by the business marketer. The typology in Table 2 suggests six buying conditions which can also be utilized for focusing BBRM tactics with the Internet. The business marketer's task is enumerated by contrasting the traditional approach with an Internet augmented approach. The discussion is ordered from least complex to most complex buying task and reveals that the Internet plays an increasing role as the buying task grows in complexity. There is a synergy with Internet augmented business buyer relationships.

Straight Rebuy (SR). A business buyer's automated repurchases are the most sought after goal for any business marketer. Retention can only be achieved through repeated communication. These *casual purchases* involve very little information search and analysis and are of minor importance to the buyer, even though some *routine low priority purchases* are somewhat more important involving a moderate amount of analysis. At the minimum, such transactions require an offer and an acceptance as well as agreeing to terms used for continuous buying cycles. The growth of e-commerce means that more and more firms will be required to sustain buyer relationships for near repetitive buying through formal continuous process systems. Business buying firms are using the Internet to streamline the purchasing process through electronic procurement systems (i.e., automated order-reorder), joining trading communities and turning to electronic trading marketplaces designed specifically for their industry (e.g., chemicals).

The sale per se, even when routinized and repetitive, periodically requires after-purchase service. Post-service sales and support are costly

TABLE 2. Buying Tasks and the Internet

Buying Task	Traditional Perspective	Internet Priorities
Casual repurchases–Straight Rebuy (no information search or analysis)	buying center *user or buyer* reorders; sales rep stays in touch	trading communities, automated reorder, e-procurement, inventory management
Routine low priority–Straight Rebuy (review options, non-outine some importance)	sales rep keeps in regular contact with *buyer; in supplier* reinforce *existing* relationships; *out supplier* tries to break buyer routine	trading market places (industry), online auctions, third party sites, offer and acceptance needed for repurchase; 24/7; self service
Simple Modified Rebuy (evaluation of a narrow set of choice alternatives)	*in supplier* must prevent or precipitate; "firstest with the mostest"; *out supplier* hold there until buyer examines alternatives	Web pages central component of offering strategy, think like users, determine product and site features, online catalog searches through "1,000's" of pages, technical data updated in real time at lower cost
Complex Modified Rebuy (a larger set of choice alternatives, criteria change)	the marketer's task is similar, but greater effort required and over a longer time frame	the marketer's task is similar and may also include use of Extranets, account tracking, supplier scorecards all with sales rep augmentation
Judgmental New Task (unfamiliar with technology, criteria and suppliers)	early stages involvement, mindful of changing needs, advantage to "first in offer" or in supplier on other items	synchronize Web with traditional strategies and one component of overall communication strategy, prospect identification and qualification
Strategic New Task (and the decision is extremely important to the firm)	careful monitoring of changing needs	cross organizational and cross functional dialogues Internet and Extranets augmented

Sources: Synthesized from the Buying Tasks part of the BUYGRID Framework (Robinson, Faris and Wind 1967), expanded by Hutt and Speh (2001). The dichotomy for the modified-rebuy and other refinements are attributable to several researchers including, but not limited to: Doyle, Woodside and Michel (1979), Ferguson (1979); Bellizzi and McVey (1983)

due to their salient characteristics of variability and intangibility. Buyer after-purchase service requests must be tracked across all departments and therefore the many faces of the buyer. There has been a shift from phone and fax-based service to email and web-based access 24/7. Yousef (2001) notes that call centers and Web-based technologies now occupy a strategic position and affect buyer relations and corporate reputation. These operations are increasingly ensconced as integral part of business buyer relationship management. This approach allows the business marketer to learn about emerging service problems, thereby an early warning system for detecting buyers who might slip into a modified-rebuy mode (i.e., reconsidering vendors or even buying criteria).

 Modified Rebuy (MR) is a business buying situation that requires business marketers sustain interest in their firm's offering, so buyer loyalty does not waver, as well as luring active buyers from competitors. The *simple modified Rebuy* involves a narrow set of choice alternatives and encompasses a moderate amount of search and analysis while the *complex modified Rebuy* involves a larger choice set and has some uncertainty for the buyer. These buying situations represent key areas for sustaining financial performance through business buyer relationship management. The focus is on keeping buyers once obtained while attracting others from competitors.

An important step in properly crafting e-business processes is providing the buyer with a single point of contact, either through the Website or through contact with one, and only one representative of the company. Barua, Konana, Whinston and Yin (2001) found that many firms have streamlined buyer-related processes with 75% of firms surveyed providing one-stop contact while 81% resolve buyer complaints with only a few steps that are often hidden from the buyer. Such resolutions help to insure business buyers will not question or wander from their quasi-automatic buying mode. Equally important for the business marketer, these internal processes should be coordinated so that a business buyer's request filtered through the contact point results in their receiving immediate assistance.

By extension, e-direct marketing also helps sustain business buyer relationships. As a form of direct response marketing it can be used for obtaining and sustaining regular buyers helping to quantifying ROI for Internet relationship-based business (Loro 1999a, p. 19). As a lowest cost structural tic, c-direct fosters the frequency of contacts at lower cost. Hence, continuous dialogue and real-time buyer service becomes viable. Lags times are forgotten, phone lines are no longer clogged and the potential for conflict is reduced making it less likely for buying firms to consider switching brands (Blankenhorn 2000, p. 30).

New Task (NT) Buyers are an ongoing part of a mature business's market development. First time buyers to a product class or a particular brand are inevitable over time. Relationship acquisition is an important part of a mature firm's strategy. The greatest level of uncertainty confronts buying firms in a *judgmental new task* situation because of the technical complexity of the product class, the difficulty in evaluating alternatives and the heightened unpredictability of unproven suppliers. *Strategic new tasks* require even more effort invested given the extreme importance of the purchase to the firm's overall well-being. In either instance, the business marketer must be able to "walk" buying center members through derivation of criteria and setting specifications given their respective emphasis on different buying criteria (Lichtenthal 1988) in this group choice-task process.

For the business marketer, filtering these prospects can be costly, but less so, if done by e-mail, Website visitor monitoring *and visiting buyers' sites* for market intelligence. Lead and opportunity management for the most qualified buying organizations, based on prior or emerging segments, can often prove useful for business marketers who want to capture new business. This approach can augment traditional sales force tele-prospecting methods (Lichtenthal, Sikri and Folk 1989) for proactive identification and screening of new accounts.

With no prior experience, a trust gap may occur given the physical separation of the seller and the buyer, the physical separations of the buyers from the seller's merchandise, and the overall perceptions of insecure transactions over the Internet (Warrington, Abgrab and Caldwell 2000). Fostering trustworthiness is required to make the initial sale. Frazier, Spekman, and O'Neal (1988) indicate that three variables enhance trust: personal integrity, upheld promises and forgone opportunistic behavior, all of which can only be determined over time. As the business buyer relationship matures and is enhanced, "past experiences" of the buyer may come to include favorable perceptions, buyer loyalty and retention. Several Websites have moved from simplistic communications objectives to a more complex continuous transactional mode. Warrington, Abgrab and Caldwell (2000) note that cues such as product guarantee, secured website transactions and alternative order processes, are important to initiating the relationships with the promise of trust.

New buyers are harder and more expensive to acquire than retained buyers and new products are harder and more expensive to sell than established products (Freidman and Furey 1999). The cure for unfocused buyer relationship management is to balance the seeking of whole new vistas of opportunity, while assessing carefully where the bulk of profitable sales growth is really located. The further a firm gets away from its core base of existing buyers and products, the more likely it will lower profitability and weaken relationships with buyers. Such incremental steps must be taken slowly while mindful of current strengths on both sides of the seller-buyer dyad.

Another area, which can be viewed as a *quasi-new task*, is "build to order manufacturing." The buyer has product class experience and brand familiarity but has decided to make their purchase with specifications not fully articulated. In order to build-to-order, companies (and their suppliers) must understand what buyers want (Holweg and Pil 2001). Product flexibility relates how well the company adapts a product to meet buyer specifications. By bringing customization closer to the buyer and managing product variety, buyers have a say in what they obtain, minimizing production and supply chain costs. A business marketing firm must not lose sight of buyer requirements as they are ever-changing.

STRENGTHENING BUSINESS BUYER RELATIONSHIPS VIA CHOICE PROCESSES

It is widely recognized that the buying process starts with "need recognition" (Robinson, Faris and Wind 1967; Johnston 1981) and eventually proceeds to set criteria ("specs") as well as evaluating and selecting alternatives. In business markets, vendors set specifications for their item(s) and with XML enabled browsers buyers can use product standards and automatically examine remote databases on the Internet for similar seller information (Oliva 2001, p. 47). Facilitation of business buyers' choice processes can be an attraction for fostering long-term relationship with value-added for the business buyer.

Evaluation Criteria: XML with standard tags means buyers can sort, search and compare across different item descriptors of one company's offering to that of another. This information can be stored or used in real-time to assemble orders and conduct other aspects of business. Business marketers need to create integrated marketing portals both within and across business buying organizations. Information can be automatically updated at the portal, when the content changes at the source. Emerging and recurring requirements can often be obtained this way.

Evaluation often requires immersion in the product genre. Deighton (2000) notes that stickiness (i.e., where people find themselves spending more time than they intended) is one possible indicator of the utility of a Website. Three dimensions emerge for providing business buyer attraction: a *social-to-individual* dimension which includes the opportunity to be with people and entice them; a *creative-to-destructive* dimension which engrosses individuals in the creative act of building something and the chance to complain, rant and vent; a *vacant-to-purposeful* dimension which involves sites that indulge in the act of spacing out. Hence the provision of "chat rooms" or "bulletin boards" for a brand or vertical marketplace may provide a basis for value-added that foster business buyer relationships in the long-term.

Introducing Touch Points: For pre-purchase evaluation, buyer relationship management also means responsible acquisition and deployment of knowledge about buyers through the cultivation of touch points (Taeschler 1999, p. 13). These include the obvious channels in the integrated communications mix as well as fewer obvious channels about how the buyer interacts with a brand (i.e., sales calls, billing records, service requests, usage). BBRM in this mode adopts a corner store approach to buyer service backed by sophisticated database technology. The business buyer must be able to connect with all aspects of the business marketer's offering while using the modality that suits its corporate resources and buying style.

ALIGNMENT OF BUSINESS BUYER RELATIONSHIP STRATEGY AND TACTICS

BBRM as Strategy: At the firm level, organizational priorities must include BBRM as part of an overall marketing strategy. In contrast, CRM is better thought of as a tactical subset of BBRM which functions beyond marketing as well (Blankenhorn 1999a, 1999b, 1999c). Data from a variety of sources must be organized and shared providing a single view of the buyer. The goal of CRM is building current loyalty fueled by high-technology (Loro1999b, p. 22). The buyer's viewpoint is that they must be able to "touch" the business marketer in a variety of modes (Michael 2001, p. 37). These touch-points for galvanizing business relationships include: two way communications for garnering feedback and reacting, providing accurate and customized response to queries, expert buyer service, a 360-degree view of the business buyer and business marketer to each other, personalized marketing techniques, and a self-service option while fostering multi-channel contact. These tactics developed for CRM can be applied to BBRM across all buying situations (i.e., SR, MR and NT).

Techniques Transcend Segments: The aforementioned techniques have in common fulfilling buyer information exchange needs as if each buyer is their own market segment-mass customization of information regardless of buying situation. All organizational facets from both sides of the seller-buyer dyad can come in contact with each other as needed. It allows the business marketer to see all the faces of the buyer as well as all the facets of the seller. Community building becomes an objective as an extension of business marketer brand identity. It is very subtle, since products as magnets generate discussions that are laden with levels of brand imagery (Ward 1999, p. 24).

Websites must encourage strong buyer interaction through various forums. With dedicated staff to develop and nurture buyer leaders and lurkers alike, an electronic community emerges around a brand and buyers' relationships to it. It should be noted that all the tasks can be now managed with one tool called either *marketing resource management* or *enterprise marketing management* (Williamson 2001) through maintaining buyer relationships on multiple fronts.

BBRM Impact on Intelligence: The next generation market research questions will focus on many themes (Barnett 2000). One focus, contrasting learning styles on-line with "real-world" learning as well as developing on-line relationships (creating genuine dialogue with on-line buyers that allows them to co-create and customize products/services). Another focus will be on-line customization and personalization including the development of very sophisticated tools including neural nets to reinforce and deepen the levels of customization. These approaches will include the recognition "fluid" online segments. The revolution in e-commerce may be dead but the evolution lives on (Sawney 2001). Early B2B forays seemed to forget that business models should be grounded by solid buyer value propositions, not fear or greed. The end-goals have never changed and never will as B2B e-commerce is a means and not an end. However, there are procedures delineating the appropriate steps for planning, managing and assessing Websites per se (Evans and King 1999).

IN CLOSING

Buyer relationship management must start with a business strategy, which drives changes in the business marketer's organization and work processes, which are in turn enabled by information technology–not the other way around. One of business marketing's next great arenas is an automated frontier that will be managed by complex software toward a broader concept known as business buyer relationship management.

A strategic goal today is being the easiest company to do business with. If you want to do more business with your partners, then business marketers must make it easier to use or sell products by being up-to-date with specs and collaterals. The easier the system is, the more opportunities there will be for relationship development and business enhancement. Business marketers need to leverage business buyer relationships, in part by providing information rich Websites. The collaborative e-business world will take more effort to achieve results with new standards like XML and the maturation of Web services. The likelihood of success increases if business marketers drive everything from a business buyer's perspective, share vital information with partners and buyers while taking a team approach. Next generation systems using secure

Extranets allow vendors and partners to exchange leads, their status and other current buyer information.

BBRM requires a buyer-centric business philosophy and culture to support effective business marketing, sales and service processes across all direct and indirect buyer interactions regardless of the channel and buyer status. Maximization of inter-enterprise relationship streams of many-to-many people across the business seller-buyer dyad is paramount. The facilitation of this tactic is incumbent upon the business marketer, not their buyer. The fundamental determinants of the success of BBRM tools will be how well they integrate sales, service as well as marketing and other functions. This will be achieved by presenting the many faces of the business buyer, to all possible touch-points, across the relationship marketing network so that the business marketers' employees and partners do their jobs with efficiency, effectiveness and at lower human and financial costs.

NOTES

1. It should be noted that all three modes can be practiced by the same buying or selling firm. The use of one mode does not preclude the use of the others: (1) concurrently or at different times; (2) or with the same or different firm. This is a characterization about the national prevalence of a business practice.

2. A review of the definition of a limit will reveal its intuitive appeal for viewing market space occupancy if we note that: $lim\ F\ (x) = L\ as\ x\ goes\ to\ a$. The closer the value of given market effort (a) approaches saturation, the closer the corresponding market function value for occupancy (x) approaches saturation as well. These may differ by as little as we please by taking values of x which are sufficiently close to a.

REFERENCES

Anderson, J. C. and J. N. Narus (1991), "Partnering as a Focused Market Strategy," *California Management Review*, 33, Spring, 96.

Barnett, S. (2000), "The Next Generation of E-Commerce Research," *The World According to E-Commerce*, K. Haberkern, K. Hubbard, W. Moe (eds.), Marketing Science Institute, Report 00-102, 37-40.

Barua, A., Whitson, S.B. and F. Yin (2001), "Diving E-Business Excellence," *Sloan Management Review*, Fall, 36-44.

Bellizzi, J. A. and P. McVey (1983). "How Valid is the Buy-grid Model?" *Industrial Marketing Management*, 12, 57-62.

Blankenhorn, Dana (1999a), "Customers help make software affordable," *Advertising Age's Business Marketing*, 84, 4, 33-34.

Blankenhorn, Dana (1999b), "CRM extends beyond marketing to fulfillment," *Advertising Age's Business Marketing*, 84, 12, 37-38.

Blankenhorn, Dana (1999c), "Entire company must apply CRM principles," *Advertising Age's Business Marketing*, 84, 12, p. 38.

Blankenhorn, Dana (2000), "Masters integrate e-mail with CRM," *Advertising Age's Business Marketing*, 85, 1, p. 30.

Barua, A., F. Konana, A. B. Whinston and F. Yin (2001), "Driving E-Business Excellence," *MIT Sloan Management Review*, Fall, 36-44.

Blattberg, R. C. and Deighton, J. (1991), "Interactive Marketing: Exploiting the Age of Address-ability," *Sloan Management Review*, Fall, 5-14.

Cannon, J. P. and W. D. Perrault (1999), "Buyer-Seller Relationships in Business Markets," *Journal of Marketing Research*, 36, 3, 439-460.

Deighton, J. (2000), "Sources of Increasing Returns on the Internet," *The World According to E-Commerce*, K. Haberkern, K. Hubbard, W. Moe (eds), Marketing Science Institute, Report 00-102, 25-27.

Doyle, P., A. G. Woodside and P. Michel (1979), "Organizational Buying in New Task and Rebuy Situations," *Industrial Marketing Management*, 8, 7-11.

Dwyer, F. R., Schurr, P. H. and Oh, S. (1987), "Developing Buyer-Seller Relationships," *Journal of Marketing*, 51, 11-27.

Evans, J. R. and V. E. King (1999), "Business-to-Business Marketing and the World Wide Web: Planning, Managing, and Assessing WEBSITES," *Industrial Marketing Management*, 28, 343-358.

Ferguson, W. (1979), "An Evaluation of the BUYGRID Analytic Framework," *Industrial Marketing Management*, 8, 40-44.

Frazier, G., Spekman, R. E. and O'Neal, C. R. (1988), "Just-in-Time Exchange Relationships in Industrial Markets," *Journal of Marketing*, 52-67.

Friedman, Lawrence G. and Timothy R. Furey (1999), *The Channel Advantage*, Butterworth & Heinmann, 15-29.

Holweg, M. and F. K. Pil (2001), "Successful Build to Order Strategies Start with the Customer," *MIT Sloan Management Review*, Fall, 74-83.

Hutt, M. D. and T. W. Speh (2001), *Business Marketing Management*, The Dryden Press.

Iacobucci, D. and J. D. Hibbard (1999), "Toward an Encompassing Theory of Business Marketing Relationships (BMRs) and Interpersonal Commercial Relationships (ICRs): An Empirical Generalization," *Journal of Interactive Marketing*, 13, 3, 13-33.

Kanter, R. M. (1994), "Collaborative Advantage," *Harvard Business Review*, 72, July-August, 96-108.

Kotler, P. and G. Armstrong (2001), *Principles of Marketing*, Ninth Edition, Prentice-Hall, Inc., Upper Saddle River, NJ.

Kropper, Steven (2001), "A retention revolution," *Mortgage Banking*, 61, 12, 54-62.

Lichtenthal, J. D. and S. Eliaz (2002), "Internet Integration in Business Marketing Tactics," *Industrial Marketing Management*, 1-7.

Lichtenthal, J. David and S. Shani (2000), "Fostering Client-Agency Relationships: A Business Buyer Behavior Perspective," *Journal of Business Research*, 49, 213-228.

Lichtenthal, J. D., S. Sikri and K. Folk (1989), "Tele-Prospecting: An Approach for Qualifying Accounts," *Industrial Marketing Management*, 18, 1, 11-17.

Lichtenthal, J. D. (1988), "Group Decision Making in Organizational Buying: A Role Structure Approach," *Advances in Business Marketing and Purchasing,* JAI Press, Inc., 119-157.

Loro, Laura (1999a), "Marketers find Internet Gives Direct New Power," *Advertising Age's Business Marketing,* 84, 2, 19-20.

Loro, Laura (1999b), "Internet Bolsters Marketers' CRM Programs," *Advertising Age's Business Marketing,* 84, 10, 22-23.

Mahadevan, A. (2000), "Business Models for Internet-Based E-Commerce: An Anatomy," *California Management Review,* 42, 4, 55-69.

McKenna, Regis (1991), *Relationship Marketing: Successful Strategies for the Age of the Customer.* Reading, MA: Addison Wesley.

Michael, Bud (2001), "10 Ways to Galvanize your Customer Relationships," *Target Marketing,* 24, 10, p. 37.

Morrow, Edwin P. (2001), "Client relationship marketing," *Financial Services Advisor,* 144, 5, 14-19.

Oliva, Ralph A. (2001), "The promise of XML," *Marketing Management,* 10, 1, 46-48.

Parvatiyar, A. and Sheth, J. N. (1997), "Paradigm Shift in Interfirm Relationships: Emerging Research Issues," in J. N. Sheth and A. Parvatiyar (eds.), *Research in Marketing,* JAI Press, Inc., Greenwich, CT: 13, 233-255.

Pine, B. J., D. Peppers and M. Rogers (1995), "Do You Want to Keep Your Customers Forever?" *Harvard Business Review,* March-April, 103-114.

Reibstein, D. J. (2000), "Who's Buying on the Internet and How Long Will They Be Loyal," *The World According to E-Commerce,* K. Haberkern, K. Hubbard, W. Moe (eds.), Marketing Science Institute, Report 00-102, 33-35.

Robinson, P. J., Faris, C. W. and Y. Wind (1967), *Industrial Buying and Creative Marketing,* Allyn and Bacon, Inc., Boston.

Sawney, M. S. (2001), "B2B E-Commerce: The Next Generation," in "B2B E Commerce," prepared by K. Hubbard, Marketing Science Institute, 01-104, 13-17.

Taeschler, D. (1999), "Best CRM practices require cultivation of touch points," *Advertising Age's Business Marketing,* 84, 12, p. 13.

Ward, Eric (1999), "How to use, not abuse, customer information gathered online," *Advertising Age's Business Marketing,* 84, 2, p. 22.

Ward, Eric (1999), "How to build community on your site and participate in others," *Advertising Age's Business Marketing,* 84, 6, p. 24.

Warrington, T. B., Abgrab, N. J. and H. M. Caldwell (2000), "Building trust to develop competitive advantage in E-business relationships," *Competitiveness Review,* 10, 2, 160-169.

Webster Jr., F. E. (1992), "The Changing Role of Marketing in the Corporation," *Journal of Marketing,* 56, October, 1-17.

Williamson, Debra Aho (2001), "New software, services help marketers automate most functions," *B to B,* 86, 17, p. 18.

Yousef, R. (2001), "Managing Customer Relationships," *New Zealand Management,* 48, 8, 39-45.

APPENDIX A

Evolving Perspectives on Business Marketing Relationships

Several marketing researchers have maintained that relationship marketing hails a paradigm shift (Parvatiyar and Sheth 1997) permanently changing the competitive playing fields for firms and their buyers (McKenna 1991). Relationships in the field of marketing operate with consensus defining qualities such as intensity, frequency of interaction, duration of the relationship and future relational expectations (Dwyer, Schurr and Oh 1987). There are several types of relationships positioned along a continuum with pure transactions and strategic alliances serving as the end points (Webster 1992; Cannon and Perrault 1999).

1. **Transactional exchanges** centers on the timely exchange of basic products as a one-time event with no prior or subsequent transactions anticipated. Repeated transactions indicate brand loyalty and recurring purchases with development of trust and credibility on the horizon.

2. **Long-term relationships** may involve contractual arrangements but managed at arms length. Sellers and buyers are somewhat pitted against each other.

3. **Seller-buyer partnerships** are characterized by reduced supplier lists, just-in-time production and associated delivery. Price and value are determined by market forces, moderated by the outcome of negotiations, based on mutual dependence and an open exchange of information.

4. **Strategic alliances** move seller and buyer toward attainment of long-term strategic goals. Alliances are formed between sellers and buyers to ensure smooth incorporation of materials into the buyer's manufacturing processes. Overall, there is a sharing of objectives to enhance each partner's competitive standing. These types of exchanges are collaborative, where sellers and buyers form strong and extensive social, economic, service and technical ties. The intent is one of lowering costs while enhancing value, thereby achieving mutually beneficial outcomes (Anderson and Narus 1991).

5. **Hybrid structures:** distinguishing three types of long-term business marketing (interdependent) relationships, Iacobucci and Hibbard (1999) note—the strongest being under the heritage of an inter-organizational phenomenon (i.e., channels); *interpersonal commercial relationships*—including salesperson and service provider to customer relationships as well as a potpourri of B to C relations; *business to consumer*—including database, direct and interactive marketing as well as one-to-one marketing (Blattberg and Deighton 1991; Pine, Peppers and Rogers 1995). Common to all three is that customer relationship management is a transcendent tactical requirement for all market types.

6. **Integration of Perspectives:** Barnett (2000) notes the relationship management curve that companies move along starts with information, then moves to knowledge, conversation, relationship and finally e-commerce in tandem with e-customer relationship management tools.

Caveat: All of these views continue to be concurrently explored and developed by various researchers. For the sake of presentation, they are discussed in a seemingly linear fashion. In part, the genesis of one approach is likely found in the prior approaches. *All* perspectives are often *appropriately* used in a variety of business markets and even concurrently by the same business marketer.

Emergent Internet Technology Applications for Relationship Marketing: A Customer-Centered View

Jon M. Shapiro

Northeastern State University

Nicholas C. Romano, Jr.

Oklahoma State University

Banwari Mittal

Northern Kentucky University

SUMMARY. In this paper we bring together the concepts of Relationship Marketing (RM) in the marketing literature and Customer Relation-

Jon M. Shapiro, PhD, is Associate Professor of Marketing, College of Business and Technology, Department of Marketing, Northeastern State University, 3100 E. New Orleans Street, Broken Arrow, OK 74014 (E-mail: SHAPIRO@NSUOK.edu).

Nicholas C. Romano, Jr., PhD, is Assistant Professor of Information Systems, College of Business Administration, Department of Management Science and Information Systems, Oklahoma State University, 700 North Greenwood Avenue, Tulsa, OK 74106-0700 (E-mail: Nicholas-Romano@MSTM.OKState.edu).

Banwari Mittal, PhD, is Professor of Marketing, Department of Management and Marketing, Northern Kentucky University, Highland Heights, KY 41099 (E-mail: MITTAL@NKU.edu).

[Haworth co-indexing entry note]: "Emergent Internet Technology Applications for Relationship Marketing: A Customer-Centered View." Shapiro, Jon M., Nicholas C. Romano, Jr., and Banwari Mittal. Co-published simultaneously in *Journal of Relationship Marketing* (Best Business Books, an imprint of The Haworth Press, Inc.) Vol. 2, No. 3/4, 2003, pp. 85-108; and: *Customer Relationship Management in Electronic Markets* (ed: Gopalkrishnan R. Iyer, and David Bejou) Best Business Books, an imprint of The Haworth Press, Inc., 2003, pp. 85-108. Single or multiple copies of this article are available for a fee from The Haworth Document Delivery Service [1-800-HAWORTH, 9:00 a.m. - 5:00 p.m. (EST). E-mail address: docdelivery@haworthpress.com].

Digital Object Identifier: 10.1300/J366v02n03_06

ship Management (CRM) in Information Systems (IS) literature to identify and assess emergent Internet-based Information Technologies (IT) that add value for consumers. We focus on the customer's perspective by identifying the key benefits consumers seek when they enter into IT-mediated interactions with sellers. We review the IS-CRM literature and identify 8 critical IT categories that have the potential for changing how buyers and sellers establish and maintain relationships in the Internet era. Subsequently, we introduce a conceptual model, which considers the nature of the consumer's involvement with sellers through emergent Internet-based technologies in juxtaposition to potential technology-based benefits to consumers. We then discuss the implications of this proposed direction. Finally, we discuss a future research agenda, which considers the use of IT in relationship management. *[Article copies available for a fee from The Haworth Document Delivery Service: 1-800-HAWORTH. E-mail address: <docdelivery@haworthpress.com> Website: <http:// www.HaworthPress.com> © 2003 by The Haworth Press, Inc. All rights reserved.]*

KEYWORDS. Information Technologies (IT), Relationship Marketing (RM), Customer Relationship Management (CRM), consumer benefits, passive, active, and interactive systems for relationship development and management

Relationship Marketing (RM) is becoming a focal concern for both marketing and Information Systems (IS) professionals. Both researchers and practitioners in each field have made considerable progress in understanding the utility of the concept and practice of RM and in devising strategies and tools for its implementation. However, developments in the two fields have evolved somewhat independently. Specifically, marketing has grappled with the characteristics and aspects of exchange that produce or influence the long-term relational nature of exchange between partners. IS professionals, on the other hand, have focused on technology and its deployment to process customer information to identify and differentiate customers by their profit potential and to automate transactions with individual customers. We believe such isolation between the two fields minimizes realization of the full potential of information technology (IT) for enhancing RM. Specifically, newer Internet and Web technologies may prove to play a pivotal role in furthering the practice of RM. The goal of this paper is to identify and describe potential Internet and Web technologies, to juxtapose them with customer benefits, and to consider how they can be utilized within different stages of the relational exchange process. In so doing, we build a bridge between the two academic disciplines of marketing and IS, and show how synergies between the efforts of the two communities can be exploited. This paper is organized as follows. First we discuss how RM has been a concern, separately, in each of the two disciplines. Then, we consider benefits consumers seek via IT-mediated relationships. Next, we survey emergent Internet-based technologies for RM and CRM. Subsequently, we develop an IT classification scheme based on buyer and seller involvement. Then, we consider how eight critical IT technologies fit into this classification scheme and how they can benefit the customer. This is followed by a discussion of which technologies are best utilized across the relationship exchange process. We conclude the paper with implications for managers and suggestions for future research.

THE EMERGENCE OF RM
IN MARKETING AND INFORMATION SYSTEMS

Researchers and practitioners in Marketing, Information Systems, and Customer Relationships are increasingly concerning themselves with establishing and maintaining long-term relationships with customers. Customers are also becoming more demanding in their expectations for quality, service, privacy, and communication with businesses. With demanding customers and consequently increasing churn among a firm's customers, marketers are now focusing on customer retention rather than revenue or market share targets. Relationship building and management have become principal modern marketing approaches in both research and practice (Dwyer, Schurr and Oh 1987) as the paradigm in marketing strategy has shifted from "*Marketing Mix*" to "*Relationship Marketing*" (RM) (Grönroos 1994).

RM emphasizes building relationships that lead to customer retention and long term customer loyalty, in contrast to traditional transactional marketing, in which making a one-time, immediate sale to the customer was the focus (Grönroos 1994). Relationship marketing realizes that the key to keeping the customer for the long haul is to offer customers benefits they seek in the marketplace and to serve customers' interests, rather than simply the marketer's profit interests.

At the same time that marketers have shifted from transactional marketing to RM, so too has the IS community recognized the importance of relationships through Customer Relationship Management (CRM). Fundamentally, CRM concerns attracting and keeping "*economically valuable*" customers while repelling and eliminating "*economically invaluable*" ones. In the IS research community, CRM grew out of Electronic Commerce (EC). Initially, the main plank of EC was EDI system (Electronic Data Interchange), a computer system linkage established between the supplier and its business customer. Using this linkage, the supplier could gain visibility into the customer's inventory movement and implement automated reordering system (Wang, Head and Archer 2000). The utility of the EDI systems remained confined to business customers, i.e., in B2B markets. Today IS research into EC and CRM has expanded considerably to include Business-to-Consumer (B2C) markets as well as other intra-organizational components such as Supply Chain Management (SCM) (Clark and Lee 2000) and has even seem some integration of Relationship Marketing (Wang, Head and Archer 2000). IS CRM research and practice is rapidly expanding in three areas: Operational, Analytical, and Collaborative (Gefen and Ridings 2002). Operational CRM attempts to provide seamless integration of back-office transactions with customer interfaces (Gefen and Ridings 2002). Analytical CRM enables an organization to analyze customer relationships through data mining (Gefen and Ridings 2002). Collaborative CRM enables organizations to communicate intimately with selected customers, suppliers, and business partners (Kobayashi et al. 1998).

The Expanding Scope of RM in Marketing and IS Research

In the past, practitioners and researchers tended to view relationship-building as more significant and valuable in the Business-to-Business (B2B) market than in the Business-to-Consumer (B2C) market, primarily due to the cost of communicating with individual customers. In contrast to the B2B market, relationship concepts have been only loosely investigated in the B2C arena and are usually based on market phenomena, such as direct sales (Sheth, Sisodia and Sharma 2000). Due to the characteristics of retail markets (e.g., mass merchandising, low cost of switching the retailer, etc.), relationships between retailers and consumers may be more difficult to build and maintain (Sirdeshmukh, Singh and Sabol 2002). Specifically, because there are typically a large number of consumers, building relationships with individual consumers has historically been an expensive and therefore infeasible proposition. With the advent of the Internet, however, these hurdles to establishing one-to-one relationships in B2C mass markets seem to be on the verge of being overcome.

Emerging Internet technologies make it feasible for firms to engage in one-to-one interactions with millions of retail consumers. Firms are adapting these technologies, but primarily as automation to achieve anticipated productivity gains. Some IT practitioners are not aware of the benefits of such technology from the marketing relationship perspective. Many IT professionals focus on CRM solely through data capture and data analysis, rather than on analyzing the benefits to customers who use new Internet technologies; however, others have begun to explore these benefits. IS researchers and practitioners have started to incorporate marketing principles, models, techniques and customer-relationship-oriented areas into CRM implementations and studies. For example, IS researchers have identified, discussed, and empirically studied several potential benefits customers may derive from CRM and relationship marketing and management including but not limited to convenience, reduced search costs and time, and delivery advantages. Wang, Head and Archer (2000) develop a relationship-building model that extends the concepts of network marketing to the Web retail marketplace. The model assumes that both marketers and consumers perform marketing functions; consumers analyze and market their needs and seek information and solutions, compare the value of alternatives, and make decisions (Wang, Head and Archer 2000). Additionally, several IS researchers have explored consumer decision support systems and the benefits and value they might offer to customers (e.g., Mathieson, Bhargava and Tanniru 1999). Analogously, marketing researchers have also identified a number of potential consumer benefits that may derive from participation in electronic markets including: increased alternatives for consideration, additional methods for screening alternatives, increased information about alternatives, lower transaction costs, and personal security (Alba et al. 1997). Continued incorporation of insights from the RM perspective could move IS research and practice further toward including the customer in the relationship management process and ensuring that customers derive value from their participation. In this context, we next discuss a set of benefits customers seek in their interactions with marketers; benefits we assert should become a component of IT-driven assessment of customer interaction technologies.

POTENTIAL BENEFITS CONSUMERS SEEK FROM IT-MEDIATED RELATIONSHIPS

Overall, the marketing concept is based on the foundation of meeting the customer's needs. What these needs are varies based on myriad contextual elements including: (1) the nature of the consumer (e.g., brand-loyal, experiential), (2) the type of product-offering (e.g., product or service), and (3) the purchasing situation (e.g., high versus low involvement).

Integrating the literature (Keeney 1999) with recognition of these contextual elements, we identify the following eight customer-based benefits, providing key dimensions (see Table 1 for definitions we derive from the literature).

Improving Product Information Search and Processing. Product information is critical for consumers to make decisions. However, consumers are generally cognitive misers and often wish to obtain the requisite information with the least effort. There are many dimensions associated with this category, including: making product comparisons; finding and using expert evaluations; easy price comparisons; getting fast feedback when bidding; knowing the best bidding techniques; and interacting with other customers. If Internet technologies can facilitate this goal, as we

TABLE 1. Potential Consumer Benefits Defined

Potential Benefit	Definitions
Improving product information search and processing	Facilitating the minimization of cognitive effort and streamlining an effective decision process and outcome.
Better prices	The amount of money charged for a product or service.
Better delivery system	Transference of a product-offering between exchange partners.
More satisfying product benefits	Broadly conceived, products are any physical or intangible benefits offered to consumers.
Less face-to-face interactions with sales staff	Interpersonal contact between the sales staff and the consumer.
Better access to customer service	Involves the identifiable, but rather intangible, activities undertaken by a seller in conjunction with the basic goods and/or service offer.
Enjoyable shopping experience	The pleasurable subjective feeling experienced by consumers in the marketplace during pre-purchase activities.
Decreased perceived risk	Any action of a consumer will produce consequences which s/he views with some amount of uncertainty.

will show they do, then those technologies, by delivering to customers new value-added benefits, can further the practice of RM.

Better Prices. Clearly, many consumers look to purchase a desired product at the lowest price possible, or select products based on the lowest price. Key dimensions associated with this benefit are: low overall product price; bypassing, or minimizing, taxes; low shipping costs; reduced transaction costs and minimal travel costs. Internet technologies allow easy price based comparisons, as we will illustrate.

Better Delivery Systems. Generally, consumers desire their product offering be delivered to them quickly, reliably, and with as few problems as possible. Additionally, having a process that facilitates easy product return is another vital component within this benefit. The following are facets associated with better distribution: fast delivery; reliable delivery; convenient return policy; and minimal traveling time and costs in product acquisition. Clearly, this benefit is best obtained via the Internet technologies for digital products such as music and electronic documents.

More Satisfying Product Benefits. Depending on the product and context, consumers seek some combination of utilitarian and symbolic benefits. They want a product that will help reinforce or shape their self-concept and one that is safe and has good functional quality. Quality, safety, and prestige are key sub dimensions of this complex and vital benefit. Since the Web puts the entire world at the consumer's fingertips, global access to products expands customers' choices manifold, thereby increasing the likelihood of the customer finding the desired product.

Less Face-To-Face Interactions with Sales Staff. Many buyers want to make their purchases in an environment where they can obtain the information they want but where they are not obligated to interact with ignorant, pushy, or rude customer sales or service personnel. This inherent advantage associated with the Internet becomes especially salient when there is perceived pressure to purchase a product. The sub-dimensions of this benefit are privacy, reduced pressure, and the ability to practice market voyeurism (referred to on the Internet as lurking).

Better Access to Customer Service. Many consumers want the ability to access product-related information at any time in order to purchase, use, or return products. Additionally, the ability to obtain real time information while placing orders is important to customers. Key dimensions associated with this benefit include: 24/7 access to information; 24/7 purchasing ability; simple and fair return policies; and prompt response to questions and requests for help. Again, 24/7 access is one of the most significant advantages of Web-based interaction.

An Enjoyable Shopping Experience. Depending on the context, for many consumers, an enjoyable shopping experience is an important benefit. This may involve being able to obtain information in an efficient, or novel way; connecting with people of similar interests; establishing a relationship with salespersons; sensation seeking; and hedonistic consumption. While the Internet is a "faceless" medium, and at first, it would consequently seem to be at a disadvantage, we argue that in fact, given the multimedia format, it can be a source of shopping enjoyment for consumers.

Decreased Perceived Risk. There are many overlapping dimensions to this benefit. People like to make a purchase without having to worry that the product will cost too much, be unsafe, embarrass them, be of inferior quality, or take too much time. The Internet has the potential of reducing perceived risk for at least 2 reasons: (a) because the offering is on a universal, global medium, there is, in many cases, less risk of some fly-by-night vendor parading shoddy merchandise, and (b) access to a global wider merchandise selection can facilitate customer confidence in his or her selection. At the same time, the Internet introduces its own set of risks, primarily concerns about privacy.

Next, we consider useful consumer-based technologies that we will later categorize and explore in terms of their ability to produce the aforementioned eight customer benefits.

SURVEY OF EMERGENT INTERNET-BASED IT FOR RM AND CRM

Based on an extensive review of the IS-CRM literature (Romano and Fjermestad 2001), we identified eight key Internet-based technology application categories. Below, we review them briefly.

In the IS (Information Systems) literature, researchers have described these technologies, but mainly in terms of the "types" of data that can be collected with these technologies and the potential information that can be generated from it. For example, Kannan, Chang, and Whinston (1998) found that electronic communities generate insights pertaining to demographics/psychographics, transaction information, attitudes/beliefs, and interaction dynamics. Bakos (1998) noted that electronic markets support personalization and customization through consumer tracking technology to identify individual consumers, information about them, such as demographics, consumer profiles, or comparison with similar consumers. However, beyond identification of the information capture and use features of various technologies, what is needed for RM is a customer-based classification of these technologies. We develop a RM and CRM IT classification scheme from the consumer's perspective. We propose that consumers participate in relationships through the level of involvement in communicating with sellers and with other consumers via these new emergent technologies. Our review of the literature on how consumers communicate to develop and maintain relationships revealed three specific levels of participation along a continuum ranging from passive to interactive. Thus we define three types of RM and CRM technologies as Passive, Active, and Interactive, based on the role the consumer plays and we explain how they serve RM and CRM goals.

PASSIVE, ACTIVE AND INTERACTIVE RM/CRM TECHNOLOGIES

Passive RM/CRM technologies gather information from "*potential*" consumers for sellers without the buyer consciously, deliberately, or through overt action, providing the information. Consumers may be aware that "*some*" information is being gathered or communicated to sellers, but they are not specifically certain of just what that information is, nor are they specifically providing the information voluntarily. Passive technologies work in the background, via a single communication channel. The consumer has little control over the potential benefits that they can derive from the seller. This type of technology can gather information about potential buyers from their browsing behavior, through cookies, from third parties or from public online sources such as Internet discussions or news groups, through data mining and through clickstream analysis technology. In some cases the information is gleaned from secondary sources or from information the consumer provided for some other purpose.

The most publicized example of "*passive*" data collection is that of DoubleClick, the nation's leading Internet advertising service, which employs cookies to identify Internet users and collect personal information without their consent as they travel around the World Wide Web and has a database of approximately 100 million "*anonymous*" profiles. Internet users are not informed or aware that they are receiving a

DoubleClick cookie unless their browser is configured to alert them or they specifically *"opt out"* through the company's Web site.

Active RM/CRM technologies gather information from *"potential"* buyers with the buyer consciously, deliberately, and through overt action providing the information. Consumers understand the nature of the information they are providing and they are sharing it voluntarily; however, the seller does not directly respond to the consumer through an ongoing discussion, but may later contact the customer for other RM/CRM purposes. Active technologies work in the foreground. This type of technology can gather information about potential buyers through such means as registration forms, provision or information in exchange for free services, product reviews and online surveys. This information is then used for RM/CRM analysis and targeted promotions. Buyer-seller communication takes place via an individual query and response; typically with the buyer providing information to the seller without expecting any further communication related to the information that is supplied.

An active example is Compaq's (now merged with Hewlett Packard) customer communities, where customers that range from novices to technical experts can collaborate to share knowledge, information, and assistance. Joining requires that customers consent to the collection and use of their forum-based information by Compaq. Compaq also informs participants that based on the forum data, they tailor-make individual promotions and combine the acquired information for trade shows and seminars.

Interactive RM and CRM technologies gather information from *"potential"* buyers for sellers through two-way communication, with both the buyer and seller consciously, deliberately, and through overt action exchanging information, either synchronously or asynchronously. Consumers are certain of what that information is, and they provide the information voluntarily. The seller communicates directly, via multiple queries and responses, with the consumer through either the same communication channel (e.g., they communicate via e-mail), or through another channel.

For example, within Ebay's Auction Site, sellers post items for sale with a minimum bid; then buyers search for items and place a bid. The bidder then receives an email confirming their bid. After the auction is over the bidders receive email indicating whether they won the item or not with instructions on how to contact the seller to finalize the sale. Prior to the sale, buyers can email the seller to ask them for additional product information and, after the auction is over to arrange for delivery and payment.

To summarize, the distinguishing factors among the 3 technologies is the nature of the communication between the buyer and seller in terms of the buyers' level of awareness, their willingness to provide information, and the directionality of the information exchange.

If the buyer is not specifically aware the seller is monitoring the information, or for what the information is being gathered, they are not necessarily willingly providing the information, and the information exchange is one-way from buyer to seller the technology application is passive. If the buyer is aware s/he is being monitored by the seller, willingly provides the information in exchange for information access or some other commodity, and the information exchange involves only a single transfer from buyer to seller, the technological application is active. However, if the buyer is aware of the monitoring and willingly engages in an ongoing, two-way discourse with the seller, the technological application is interactive.

CLASSIFICATION
OF THE IDENTIFIED TECHNOLOGIES BY TYPE

We classify emergent technologies as passive, active, or interactive and then we evaluate them based upon the eight consumer-based benefits (see Table 2). Space does not permit a full discussion of all the technologies, but salient features of the classification are discussed below. Therefore, we discuss selected technologies below to serve as an illustration of the principal theme of this paper–how various technologies can offer customer benefits conducive to building relationships. Clearly, each of the technologies can be used by sellers within any participation mode (passive, active, or interactive), as they are extremely flexible; however, we will provide examples of the most common ways in which they are utilized.

Benefits Associated with Selected Emergent Technologies

Passive Technologies

Cookies are small text files a merchant whose Web site a consumer accesses leaves on the consumer's computer disk space. This cookie file contains a record of the consumer's click stream (i.e., the pages the con-

TABLE 2. Consumer Benefits Delivered by Emergent Internet Technology Applications

	1 Improved Information Search	2 Better Prices	3 Better Delivery Systems	4 More Satisfying Product Benefits	5 Less Face-To-Face Interactions with Sales Staff	6 Better Access to Customer Service	7 An Enjoyable Shopping Experience	8 Decreased Perceived Risk
Passive								
Cookies	x			x				
Active								
Chat Rooms (Hosted by Seller)	x			x		x	x	x
Forums (Hosted by Seller)	x			x				x
Recommender Software	x	x						x
Interactive								
E-mail	x	x				x		x
Forums (Hosted by Seller, Who Interactively Participates)	x			x		x		x
Auctions		x			x		x	x
Online Trade Shows	x	x	x	x	x	x	x	x

sumer viewed on the merchant's site). Also, it records any information the consumer may have provided the merchant while online, such as name, address, and credit card number, etc. This cookie file is automatically sent back to the merchant's computer, due to a built-in request in the file, whenever the consumer revisits the merchant.

Cookies help relationships through offering the consumer a number of benefits. First, more efficient information searches are possible because, based on the stored information regarding the buyer's demographics, past purchasing and information-gathering behavior, the seller is able to lead customers to more relevant and useful information consistently and efficiently. Second, it is possible for the consumer to obtain more befitting product benefits. Through cookies, the seller better understands the customer's preferences and is more likely to steer her toward more suitable product offerings. For example, Travelocity. com is a Web site that implements cookies to track the user's origin and destinations. Thus, when entering the site, the vendor knows the user's name, what destinations s/he is most likely to be interested in, preferences regarding airlines and fairs and favorite hotels. This makes the search more efficient for the consumer and she is likely to be steered toward trips that are appropriate.

Active Technologies

Chat rooms (hosted by seller). This technology application has revolutionized the way customers can communicate with each other. Chat rooms have made it possible for people with shared interests to come together, from any geographic area, anonymously, and communicate about a product offering in *real time*. This technology is active for two reasons. Within many seller hosted chat rooms and forums, the seller monitors the information in order to develop an appropriate product-offering, but *does not* interactively participate within the conversations. Furthermore, this variant of the chat room is mostly utilized among buyers and/or professionals. For example, prohealth.com is a physician and healthcare-recruiting agency, which sponsors a chat room for healthcare professionals to discuss issues associated with their profession such as professional conduct and job acquisition knowledge. Consumers can share product related information at Webhealthcentre. com where they can discuss and find the most suitable product for their condition.

This technology application helps the customer perform information search and obtain a better product offering (e.g., a superior value, price and service), thus lowering perceived risk. If a consumer is able to find an active chat room, s/he may be able to get feedback regarding a product faster than from any other technological channel. Given the informal nature of most chats, for some consumers, this leads to an enjoyable experience where people with similar interests can be met.

Forums (hosted by seller) comprise a complex technological application category. Overall, forums, news groups, and other online discussion serve the same purpose as chat rooms, but with slightly different features and functions. These are asynchronous ways of communicating, as opposed to chats, which are live and synchronous. They offer more detailed information than chats and a record of an ongoing conversation that can be searched. Chats typically do not offer this record and they are far less formal. Similar to chat, across many of such forums, the sellers observe the communiqués but do not participate directly within the conversations. There are primarily two types of host-sponsored forums. With the first less common variant, the sponsor hosts the forum with clients and a firm-employed expert who answers questions. This is interactive by nature. With the second, more common form, buyers register to enter and are aware the firm is monitoring the discussions.

Customers typically utilize this technology application to solve product-related problems. For example, Peoplesoft sponsors a forum within their Web site *(www.peoplesoftfans.com/forums)* so users can come together and determine how to develop solutions. It is also used to post resumes, job listings, and for bringing people with common special interests together.

The primary benefit to customers is that information is easier to obtain and people looking to solve similar problems can pool resources. This facilitates site loyalty, as people tend to visit such forums repeatedly. As a result of unbiased information and opinion from other users gleaned from these platforms, consumers are more likely to buy the correct product and determine the vendor who has the best offering and service.

Recommender Software Systems. This technological application is active in that the buyer may first contact the firm and purchase a product via e-mail, and the seller will then change the Web-based information the buyer receives regarding future purchase recommendations. Key advantages of this technology application are the facilitation of the buying process by helping customers to find the product they wish to purchase and improving cross-selling by recommending additional products or services based on customer's individual preference profiles. Overall, this technology application enables the customer to conduct an efficient information search and choose a suitable product within a chosen context. The consumer can also review product evaluations from experts and fellow customers who are past buyers. For example, reel.com provides film reviews from popular critics as well as from viewers. It also presents user-based evaluations based on demographics (e.g., age and gender). Thus, the potential buyer can see what her peers think about the product. Amazon.com provides personalized recommendations based on the site visitor's past purchases and information searches. Additionally, the site provides product evaluations by experts (e.g., book reviewers), as well as past buyers across myriad product categories (e.g., books, electronics, DVDs, music, software, magazine subscriptions).

Benefits to consumers are many. This technology application simplifies information search and feedback from experts as well as other buyers reduces perceived risk. It is also easier to find the best price and ascertain the reliability of the seller. This helps improve relationships with chosen Web sites because the consumer is likely to return when considering future purchases. This is especially true for product categories that are generally associated with repeat purchasing (e.g., books and music). When perceived risk is lowered, and this is confirmed via a positive purchase experience, consumers are likely to revisit a Web site as trust is developed.

Interactive Technologies

E-mail is the classic interactive technological application. When buyers visit Web sites, they often register in order to obtain interactive e-mail information such as newsletters, announcements, and promotions. While registration is active by nature, the process of e-mail communication is interactive. Many firms such as airlines regularly send e-mail to customers to offer them special prices and deals. Some companies, such as ListEnvoy, help firms develop their Web site so it is easy to compile visitor lists and send out e-mails.

In general, the benefit to the customer is the opportunity to obtain product information and special prices. When e-mails are sent that customers find to be useful, they are more likely to visit the sponsor's Web site to find additional benefits. When there are problems with the product, shipping, or specialized information is needed, this technology application makes it easier to communicate with the seller.

Customer relationships can be enhanced because people feel valued when given superior prices, and for some it becomes easier to obtain promotional information via this mode, given their busy schedules. This interactive technology application has changed the nature of customer service, as it is possible to get questions answered quickly, inexpensively and throughout the day.

Forums (hosted by the selling firm, in which they interactively participate). This is interactive when experts who are sellers have ongoing discussions with buyers. Product users utilize this technology application to share information, search for information, and solve product related problems. When a consumer has either a brand-specific, or product-specific question, the seller can interact in problem solving and help educate forum members about the product's virtues. This can help improve product perceptions. The primary advantage of seller-hosted interactive forums is that they provide information from experienced consumers regarding products and prices among firms vying for their business. For example, Microsoft, Inc. provides subscribers the opportunity to discuss usage related issues associated with firm employed experts to help customers solve user-related problems.

Overall, consumers benefit from participation in forums because it helps improve their knowledge about the product, they tend to purchase the product that benefits them the most, they reduce their perceived risk because they purchase after communicating with a number of experts, and they receive credible information directly and interactively from the seller.

Auctions provide consumers the opportunity to bid on products. Many auctions are interactive in that, before or during the bidding process, buyers can communicate with sellers via e-mail or chat to gain product knowledge. In other words, via the auction, buyers and sellers can conduct query and response sessions across one channel of communication. The online auction provides buyers the freedom from having to make snap decisions and rush into a purchase. The traditional method of selling typically uses the rule of *"first come first served."* For example, in the past, in real estate, if a buyer was not the first person to make an offer on a property, s/he might as well have been the last. Now, if buyers see a house listed on Rbuy.com, they do not have to be first to bid on the house, but instead place bids anytime while bidding is open (typically, for a few days or weeks). This provides the potential customer time to find an appealing house, time to inspect it, and time to research the appropriate price to pay for it. Auctions also help create a level playing field for buyers who now have access to top properties that, in the past, would have been sold before they reached the market.

This interactive platform has a number of customer-based benefits including: convenience; variety of selection; the consumer being able to determine the price s/he wishes to pay; low-pressure buying in that there are no salespeople trying to sell you things you don't want; and the consumer determining what products s/he wishes to look for to buy. Many customers also enjoy the excitement of the bidding process and the real time feedback. They think auctions are a pleasant and exciting way to buy. There is no haggling over price, so for some this is more fun and less stressful than other forms of shopping. Many bidders like the competitive spirit; they do not simply buy a product, they *win* it. For buyers, there is the lure of the potential bargain. The chance of getting a bargain adds to the fun and excitement. These benefits make customers seek the same auction sites again, thus producing relationship and loyalty.

Virtual trade shows. These are similar to conventional trade shows except that they are organized in the Internet space. Just like the conventional trade shows, there are exhibit booths, where various vendors display their products. Virtual trade shows are designed to allow buyers and sellers to have interactive conversations just like at real trade shows, however these may be via e-mail, chat or telephone. For example itradeFair.com has technology that enables customers at a trade show to click on a special link in a trade show booth that causes both their phone and that of the vendor to ring simultaneously so they can have a live interactive conversation, enabling customers to discuss the booth and the products in real time just as if they were at a trade show.

The advantage to customers is that they can "visit" the trade shows anytime from anywhere, without having to travel to the exhibit site and without getting tired feet. It provides visitors an opportunity not only to discover what various products and services are available, but also to interact with manufacturers and suppliers instantaneously by e-mail to request further information or to place an order. Thus, the most significant advantage of this Web tool to customers is that it offers information about new products to be gathered without the usual search costs. Since the trade show focuses on a particular industry, information about multiple vendors can be obtained all in one click on a single site. Since the vendors are demonstrating their newest products, it enables customers to stay informed on the latest developments in the industry. Product attributes can be compared to identify the product and vendor with the most suitable set of product benefits. Also, digital product samples are delivered easily–you place samples in your exhibit cart and the contents are e-mailed to you, thus facilitating distribution. There is freedom from any unpleasant interpersonal interaction, and browsing through the trade show, viewing animated demonstrations of new products and solutions can be an enjoyable experience.

The advantage to the company is exposure to worldwide customers at a fraction of the cost; in fact, the same "virtual" salesperson can demonstrate the product simultaneously to thousands of customers.

This interactive application helps customer relationship building on several counts. First, customers interact voluntarily and extensively, increasing their involvement with the vendor and his or her products. Second, customers receive the benefits without the usual search costs. Third, the enjoyable experience creates pleasant memory and associations with the vendor. Given these valued outcomes, customers would naturally like to patronize the vendor participating in the virtual trade show rather than a competitor not using this medium.

While it is interesting to consider consumer-based benefits associated with Internet technology applications, it is important for managers to understand how to employ them during the relationship formation process. Below, we consider where the various Internet technologies (passive, active and interactive) can be deployed by marketers during the various stages of the relationship development.

RELATIONSHIP STAGES AND TECHNOLOGICAL MODE

Relationship marketing literature has identified five stages of relationship development: awareness, exploration, expansion, commitment, and dissolution (Dwyer, Schurr and Oh 1987). Table 3 below considers the utilization of Web-based technology applications across each relationship stage as either a primary or a secondary tool. During *Stage 1, Awareness*, Party A has not yet recognized that Party B is a possible exchange partner. Here, we believe the manager's use of passive technology (i.e., cookies) is most appropriate. Central to this stage is Party A's (the customer's) need for good information which is seen as beneficial. Party B's (the seller's) goal is to provide this information to as many different potential customers as possible (Party A), in an effective and efficient manner, in order to facilitate awareness across all potential exchange partners. If the customer receives useful information that is tailor-made based upon browsing behavior, hasn't been hounded for information previously from a party s/he has no current relationship

TABLE 3. Role of Emergent Internet Technology Applications at Various Relationship Stages

	1 Awareness	2 Exploration	3 Expansion	4 Commitment	5 Dissolution
Passive					
Cookies	X			X	X
Active					
Chat Rooms (Hosted by Seller)		X	X	X	
Forums (Hosted by Seller)		X	X	X	
Recommender Software		X			
Interactive					
E-mail		X	X	X	X
Forums (Hosted by Seller, Who Interactively Participates)		X	X		
Auctions		X	X		
Online Trade Shows		X	X	X	

X = Primary Tool (bold faced); X = Secondary Tool (regular faced).

with, and many customers are contacted, the seller will maximize product-offering awareness. This tailor-made communiqué can increase selective attention among individual customers. Additionally, it can reach many consumers because the seller is not limited by having to ask each potential customer for specifications prior to developing its promotional message.

In *Stage 2, Exploration*, potential exchange partners consider the costs benefits and obligations associated with a potential relationship. This stage consists of the sub-stages of attraction communication/bargaining, norm development and expectations development, and here clearly, two-way communication is vital. Both potential dyadic partners should communicate overtly in order to weigh perceived cost/benefits ratios. We believe that during exploration, Party B (seller) should primarily employ interactive technologies, because they provide 2-way interaction via the same channel. As a secondary tool, active technologies can be used to provide additional value because they can facilitate overt communication, and provide Party A with additional insight. For example, e-mail can be used to communicate norms, expectations and to develop an understanding. Similarly, the use of online trade shows can suggest to the customers/visitors what types of benefits and costs are associated with a potential relationship. Then, by using active technologies such as forums, the customer can obtain more information from other users within the product category that can be useful when assessing the seller. However, trust is best developed when communication between the buyer and the seller is interactive.

Stage 3, Expansion, is characterized by increasing interdependence. This stage entails the same stage 2 (exploration) sub-stages (attraction, communication/bargaining, norm development and expectations development), but mutual trust is becoming deeper. While the primary deployment of interactive technologies is still central, the increasing use of active technologies is appropriate. This is because Party A (customer) is now more likely willing to disclose self-information using more active technologies. For example, if a seller provides a forum for its customers to post problems and solutions, this information could be used to develop better products and to communicate better to the buyers. This additional technological mode becomes more useful because the dyadic relationship is now in place.

Stage 4, Commitment, is characterized by a promise or agreement to continue the exchange relationship. Here, while 2-way interactive technology is still the most important mode, we believe that all 3 forms can be used in a complimentary way. As in previous stages, interactive technologies such as e-mail can be used to keep communication open, and bypass any misunderstandings.

Passive technologies such as cookies can be useful to facilitate solidarity and cohesion. For example, Party A (e.g., buyers), can obtain information via newsletters (that are cookie-generated) and not feel compelled to have to respond every time. During expansion, this mode may be less appropriate because the objective is to deepen trust, via interactive communication, rather than simply maintain contact. Active technology is still useful because committed people may want to communicate with others in similar situations to share problem-solving strategies. For instance, the seller can host a forum in order to facilitate user-related problem solving, so buyers might have to anticipate future roadblocks in order to help improve the product offering. Interactive technologies such as e-mails can also help facilitate commitment. For instance, many airlines send special newsletters to their most frequent flyers providing them special e-mails, containing promotional incentives in order to encourage brand loyalty. The customers are encouraged to communicate directly with the airline in order to obtain richer product information.

Stage 5, Dissolution, is what most marketers generally strive to avoid. However, upon entering this stage, interactive technology is vital as fast two-way interactions between the buyer and seller become vital. Secondarily, in some situations, passive technologies may also be useful, as Web-based behaviors can be monitored through cookies. For instance, via cookies, Party A (the marketer) may determine which competitor's sites Party B (the customer) is visiting and tailor the subsequent message accordingly to show the correct product benefits. Thus, it is through the process of obtaining cookie-related intelligence that the seller could develop a communiqué designed to defer the dissolution.

CONCLUSION AND DISCUSSION

Implications for Marketing and IS Researchers and Practitioners

With the rapid proliferation of emergent Internet technology applications, it becomes essential for researchers to develop a classification system, to aid the in the IT selection process with the goal of optimizing relationship management. It is important for firms to be cognizant of the different relationship-based benefits that consumers seek, and of which Internet technology applications have the potential to deliver these benefits. Being oblivious to some of these benefits, and not considering them when developing Web site applications, may result in lost opportunity. For example, if a firm fails to leverage its technological assets to lessen customer's perceived risk (e.g., by utilizing forums to answer usage-related issues, or interactive e-mails to help alleviate fears), it may unknowingly alienate customers and decrease repeat purchases.

We have identified 8 emergent technology applications in 3 categories, passive, active, and interactive. Each category implies a specific mindset for the consumer, and as a result entails unique issues for the seller to consider.

Active technologies entail the customer voluntarily participating so s/he is inherently likely to be involved and motivated. Such motivation implies a psychological link of the buyer with the seller. As obvious as this sounds, many Web sites fail to utilize active technologies. For example, many smaller booksellers fail to host forums for customers to share ideas while this is integral within some of the market leaders (e.g., Amazon.com).

With interactive technologies, the firm has the ability to respond, in real time, back to the consumer. This provides great opportunities for relationship building but can also be problematic for the firm if the customers' questions/comments are answered too slowly, inadequately, or not at all. Sadly, many firms are forgoing the distinctive features of this technology, as they are not taking advantage of customer interactions within their Web sites. Few firms provide any direct linking, via e-mail with their customers, or fail to respond in a timely fashion.

Passive technology has the inherent disadvantage that the consumer is not choosing it; however, if well managed, it can provide a lot of value to the customer. Of crucial importance, the selling firm is, based on information captured via passive technologies, able to deliver customized information and offerings. Since the customer did not seek out promotional messages, the firm using passive technology should make sure that the offers and messages are of value to the consumer. Thus, it is vital that the firm scrutinize its content to be sure it is relevant, easy to understand and fun to read. Additionally, because with passive technology, consumers do not chose to participate, the issue of privacy becomes especially relevant. The firms employing passive technologies must take the extra steps to assure privacy and proper information utilization procedures.

Finally, we have proposed how various technology applications are more, or less useful across different stages of the relationship-development process. It is important for firms to understand all customers and potential customers and determine where they currently are within the stages. Subsequently, the firm may consider tailoring the message and feedback through use of the application appropriate to the relationship-based stage the customer is in.

Contributions and Future Research Directions

We hope to draw interest from academics and practitioners alike in the development of a method to consider which configuration of Internet technology applications are most appropriate, based on consumer-based contextual variables.

Our goal in this paper was to bring together the concepts in the Marketing and IS fields together to explore the potential of Internet technology applications for further customer relationship building. Toward this goal, we have proposed a contingency profile between the set of benefits customers seek and the capabilities of various Internet technology applications classified as passive, active, and interactive. We have also proposed a contingency profile between these technologies and the stages of relationship development. We would not be presumptuous to suggest that the contingencies we propose are comprehensive, much less that they are unarguable. Rather, we view them as a reasonable first approximation, as a basis for further research. It is vital for researchers to understand how IT affects consumers. Thus, a future research path could consider which technological configurations maximize consumer-based benefits, while minimizing their detriments. Along with consumer involvement, as this paper considers (e.g., passive, active, and interactive), empirical research is needed that examines the relationship between consumer benefits sought and the emergent IT tools. Finally, research on how IT can be used to improve trust is important given this appears to be a vital attribute that is on the wane.

Our work calls for further research on a number of fronts. First, the contingencies we proposed need to be streamlined and validated, possibly with customer research–are the benefits we attribute to various technologies indeed so perceived by consumers who have experienced those technologies? Second, a cost-benefit of each technology application, and the resulting customer loyalty, which technology applications are cost effective and which are not. As we mentioned before, IT managers no doubt assess all technology on cost-benefits, but such assessment must take into account customer benefits we have outlined, and its resulting customer relationship enhancement payoffs. Third, we focused on eight selected technologies, and future research needs to expand the scope to include applications both currently available (e.g., Group Support Systems approaches to Internet focus groups and Interactive Online Interviews), and those under development (e.g., Observation Studies through Virtual Reality and Simulated Environments). Finally, we hope our effort promotes more cross-disciplinary work between marketing and IS researchers.

REFERENCES

Alba, Joseph W., John Lynch, Barton Weitz, Chris Janiszewiski, Richard Lutz, Alan Sawyer and Stacy Wood (1997), "Interactive Home Shopping: Consumer, Retailer, and Manufacturer Incentives to Participate in Electronic Marketplaces," *Journal of Marketing*, 61(3), pp. 38-53.

Bakos, Yannos (1998), "The Emerging Role of Electronic Marketplaces on the Internet," *Communications of the Association for Computing Machinery*, 41 (8), pp. 35-42.

Clark, Theodore H. and Ho G. Lee (2000), "Performance, Interdependence and Coordination in Business-to-Business Electronic Commerce and Supply Chain Management," *Information Technology & Management Journal*, 1 (1-2), pp. 85-105.

Dwyer, F. Robert, Paul H. Shurr and Seju Oh (1987), "Developing Buyer and Seller Relationships," *Journal of Marketing*, 51 (2), pp. 11-27.

Gefen, David and Catherine M. Ridings (2002), "Implementation Team Responsiveness and User Evaluation of Customer Relationship Management: A Quasi-Experimental Design Study of Social Exchange Theory," *Journal of Management Information Systems*, 19 (1), pp. 47-69.

Grönroos, Christian (1994), "From Marketing Mix to Relationship Marketing. Toward a Paradigm Shift in Marketing," *Management Decision*, 32 (2), pp. 4-20.

Kannan, P. K., Ai-Mei Chang and Andrew B. Whinston (1998), "Marketing Information on the I-Way: Data Junkyard or Information Gold Mine?" *Communications of the ACM*, 41 (3), pp. 35-43.

Keeney, Ralph L. (1999), "The Value of Internet Commerce to the Customer," *Management Science*, 45 (4), pp. 533-542.

Kobayashi, Makoto, Masahide Shinozak, Takashi Sakairi, Maroun Touma, Shahrokh Daijavad and Catherine Wolf (1998), "Collaborative Customer Services Using Synchronous Web Browser Sharing," *Proceedings of the ACM 1998 conference on computer supported cooperative work*, ACM Press, New York, NY, USA, pp. 99-109.

Mathieson, Kieran, Mukesh Bhargava, and Mohan Tanniru (1999), "Web-Based Consumer Decision Tools: Motivations and Constraints," *Electronic Markets*, 9 (4), pp. 274-277.

Romano, Nicholas C., Jr. and Jerry Fjermestad (2001), "Customer Relationship Management Research: An Assessment of Research," *International Journal of Electronic Commerce*, 6 (3), pp. 59-111.

Sheth, Jagdish N., Rajendra S. Sisodia and Arun Sharma (2000), "The Antecedents and Consequences of Customer-Centric Marketing," *Journal of the Academy of Marketing Science*, 28 (1), pp. 55-66.

Sirdeshmukh, Deepak, Jagdip Singh and Barry Sabol (2002), "Consumer Trust, Value, and Loyalty in Relational Exchanges," *Journal of Marketing*, 66 (1), pp. 15-37.

Wang, Fang, Milena Head, and Norm Archer (2000), "A Relationship-Building Model for the Web Retail Marketplace," *Internet Research*, 10 (5), pp. 374-384.

Index

For Product Safety Concerns and Information please contact our EU
representative GPSR@taylorandfrancis.com
Taylor & Francis Verlag GmbH, Kaufingerstraße 24, 80331 München, Germany

www.ingramcontent.com/pod-product-compliance
Ingram Content Group UK Ltd.
Pitfield, Milton Keynes, MK11 3LW, UK
UKHW021112180425
457613UK00005B/53